A Teenager's Dream

Why Do Fools Fall in Love:
Frankie Lymon and The Teenagers

Jimmy Merchant

Pearly Gates Publishing LLC
INSPIRING CHRISTIAN AUTHORS TO BE AUTHORS

Pearly Gates Publishing, LLC, Harlem, GA (USA)

A Teenager's Dream
Why Do Fools Fall in Love:
Frankie Lymon and The Teenagers

Copyright (c) 2023
Jimmy Merchant

Disclaimer: This book was written by the author's memory. He has done his best to be faithful and true to his experiences, and when possible, has consulted others who were also present during that time. The publisher assumes no responsibility for details, suggestions, or information contained in this book that may prove libel.

First Edition. Printed in the United States of America.

Scripture references are used with permission via Zondervan at Biblegateway.com. Public Domain.

Paperback ISBN 13: 978-1-948853-65-1
Digital ISBN 13: 978-1-948853-66-8
Library of Congress Control Number: 2023908452

For information and bulk ordering, contact:
Pearly Gates Publishing, LLC
Angela Edwards, CEO
P.O. Box 639
Harlem, GA 30814
BestSeller@PearlyGatesPublishing.com

DEDICATION

This book is lovingly dedicated to
my parents,

James and Elsie Merchant.

Their love and leadership were
instrumental in the fulfillment of my
"DREAM."

ACKNOWLEDGMENTS

I cannot thank **GOD** enough for how He operates in our lives—not only by directing us to see things from His perspective but also to bless us along life's journey. For me, it all began with a 'dream' that led to global fame at age 15 along with Joe Negroni, Herman Santiago, Sherman Garnes, and, of course, Frankie Lymon.

A special thank you to my beautiful, God-sent, second wife, **Mary Merchant**, whom I met over 30 years ago at Christian Cultural Center in Brooklyn, New York; her two children, **Adriene and Kevin,** who refer to me as their dad; and our adopted daughter, **Lisa**.

Thank you to my darling sisters, **Gigi, Jean, Alice,** and **Gail** and their children; my beautiful oldest daughter, **Victoria**, from Vickie Burgess, and my five incredible children from my first wife, Barbara: **James Jr., Jamise, Scott, Solideen**, and **Star**.

Thank you to the great pastors whom God placed in my life throughout the years: **A.R. Bernard, Deacon Holmes, Kevin Francis, Gary Miller, Mr. and Mrs. Clinton and Sarah Utterbach**, and **Dr. Bente,** my first pastor from the Bronx.

Finally, I'd like to thank **all my fans worldwide**, some of whom cannot wait to read this book, including my darling cousin **Olivia**.

For those whose names were not mentioned here, please charge it to my head and not my heart. I love and appreciate you all!

WHAT OTHERS ARE SAYING...

My grandfather, James "Jimmy" Merchant, was a superstar in my eyes long before I was old enough to fathom the magnitude of his career's impact on music, Black culture, and the world. His star quality isn't just because of his many accolades, the number of records he's sold, and the momentous mark in history he's made. It's also his smooth baritone voice, the poise in which he carries himself, his infectious laugh, and, most importantly, his otherworldly glow that can only come from a deep love of God. I remember the first time I saw my granddad perform on stage. Although his music didn't resemble the rap lyrics my friends and I liked to dance to, I was in awe. He had such a command of the stage and the crowd. I watched as an audience of fans were just as zealous about my grandfather as I was about the teenage heartthrobs I idolized on TV. That was the moment I realized that beyond what my grandfather meant to me; he also meant something special to the world. Grandpa inspired me to be an artist. Seeing him in my proximity allowed me to know it was possible. He also inspired my passion for Christ and let me know that my love for Jesus does not have to be compromised just because I'm in the entertainment industry. The Teenagers were America's first boy band and the first teenage act. Both carry an unfathomable magnitude that, unfortunately, has been buried in history. Sadly, the price of being innovators came with the burden of existing during a time when artists—especially Black artists and, more specifically, kids—did not have the rights to their original works and were sorely taken advantage of. Through this book, the truth is finally being shared with the world and is a major step in restoring my grandfather and the other legendary Teenagers to their rightful place in history.

Tationna Bosier

♫♫♫♫♫

Jimmy Merchant is a musical original and a major influence on early Doo-Wop music and the revolutionary change in Pop music during the 1950s. The music industry agrees, as evidenced by him and his group, "Frankie Lymon and The Teenagers," being inducted into the Rock and Roll Hall of Fame. Music is just one of Jimmy's creative contributions and talents. He is also a superb portrait painter. As an original member of Frankie Lymon and The Teenagers, Jimmy was the group's creative force—elements of which are heard in the songs and styles of many other groups today. For me, as a kid growing up in Brooklyn, New York, in the 1950s, Doo-Wop/R&B was the original mainstream revolutionary change in Pop music—so different from the musical styles of people like Perry Como and Rosemary Clooney, popular with White audiences at that time. Jimmy and his Teenagers group produced hit after hit. Their musical influence was at least as powerful or perhaps more powerful than the music of other pioneers of early Rock 'n Roll, such as Elvis Presley, Chuck Berry, Fats Domino, and Little Richard. I remember getting into trouble in junior high school by my Spanish teacher for passing a newly-purchased 45 rpm record of The Teenagers' *I Want You to Be My Girl* to some of my classmates—my first purchased 45 rpm and first negative brush with school officials. It was worth it to show off my new Teenagers record. Jimmy comes from modest beginnings as a kid on the streets of New York. His success happened early in his life when he was a kid…a teenager. He and his Teenagers group quickly became world famous, with global hit after hit. They performed overseas, appeared in movies and on TV, and were heard on the radio. His group had the kind of success countless others could only dream about, and it came to Jimmy and his group when they were just kids! The sad yet significant part of his story is how Jimmy and the others in his group were taken advantage of—financially and otherwise—by the powers that be in the record industry. To this day, Jimmy's religious beliefs have guided and supported him through those trials and tribulations. He manages to remain calm (I suspect in large part because his

Christian faith has given him a clear and righteous path). He walks the spiritual walk minute by minute, day by day. Overall, Jimmy is one-of-a-kind—a man who has a meaningful life story to tell about his early years on the streets of New York, his influence on early Rock 'n Roll, and how his religious beliefs have given him the strength to deal with the ebb and flow of life. I am proud to consider Jimmy Merchant my friend.

Richard Hirschman

♫ ♫ ♫ ♫ ♫

Jimmy Merchant of the original "The Teenagers" youth vocal group and creator of the '50s hit song *Why Do Fools Fall in Love* is a man of character and charm, with an immense love for God. It never ceases to amaze me how Jimmy remains humble, despite the countless injustices within the group and the music industry as a whole. Even in the most trying times when the group failed him, especially now that there are only two living original members (Herman Santiago and himself), Jimmy still supported the idea of a reunion that Herman didn't welcome, based on the poor management of his own accord. I know Jimmy Merchant as a God-fearing man whose calling is to share his gift and talent with the world without prejudice or malice and educate others regarding music and its significance. I was privileged to honor him with an impromptu performance at the Goodfellas Do-Wop and More Club in Queens, New York, with a couple known as "Stiletto and The Saxman." Doreen (who has the Frankie Lymon sound) sang *Why Do Fools Fall in Love* with Jimmy, and the video of that performance went viral. I find it challenging to understand how the other living original member can base his credibility on the Rock and Roll Hall of Fame without crediting Jimmy Merchant for his vast contributions as a crucial member of the group. Not only is Jimmy an important factor, but he is also very knowledgeable and can educate the public about the group's legendary history dating back to the mid-1950s. I have and always will believe Jimmy Merchant is a prominent, influential, and vital piece of history as an original member of The Teenagers.

Jackie Nuñez

♫ ♫ ♫ ♫ ♫

Music has three conditions: spiritual, secular, and sinful. Spiritual music encompasses praising God, loving one another, being kind, and always being mindful of our words. Secular music is simply "the world's music" and can be uplifting, informative, or merely factual. Those two conditions of music do not have to be and should not be in conflict. Sinful music has characteristics all to itself. It is harmful, denigrating, and meant to destroy the listener. That was the first lesson Jimmy Merchant taught me. I'll never forget that day... My brothers — Reginal Polk and Lloyd Ivey — and I were scheduled to perform at a festival in Somerset County, Maryland. I didn't really know who Jimmy Merchant was and, initially, was not impressed. We expected a musical performance from him, but he didn't sing or perform. Instead, he told the story of a legendary group called "Frankie Lymon and The Teenagers." Of course, we all knew who they were! The thing is this: Jimmy told the story so vividly, everyone was captivated, including me — Mr. Skepticism! He shared with the audience the story of letters that were given to his teenage group and how one of them was crafted by him into the hit song *Why Do Fools Fall in Love*. The song was first written as a ballad but was rearranged to accommodate Frankie Lymon's up-tempo style. History was made — one that would reshape the music industry by that teen group being the first boy band. When Jimmy finished speaking, I thought to myself, "Man, I have to meet this cat!" I introduced myself to him and, from the very beginning, I felt a connection. He was humble, knowledgeable, Godly, and just a cool cat. From that day forward, he became one of my very best friends, a mentor, and a father figure (seeing that my own father had passed away years before).

His knowledge of the music business, music theory, and (most importantly) the human equation is remarkable! He has lived all aspects of life and continues to be my friend, brother, and true music legend, arranger, producer, performer, guitarist, and vocalist. His name is Mr. James "Jimmy" Merchant.

Homer T. Williams, Jr.

♫ ♫ ♫ ♫ ♫

Frankie Lymon and The Teenagers is the vocal youth group that started it all! If it weren't for them, there would be no kiddy groups to follow in their footsteps, much like Lewis Lymon followed in his brother's footsteps with his group called Lewis Lymon and The Teenchords (*Lewis was good, but Frankie had a stronger voice*). The youth movement in music started with four kids from the Washington Heights area of Manhattan, New York. Jimmy Merchant was given a love note that he made into the song, *Why Do Fools Fall in Love*. Once Frankie Lymon joined the group, the rest of the story is Doo-Wop history. I've followed Frankie Lymon and The Teenagers since first being introduced to Doo-Wop. I was in middle school at the time but still listen to '50s Doo-Wop music today. In my opinion, today's music is nothing like it was in the '50s. Heck no! As a matter of fact, during my daily walk, my choice of music is from that era. I had the pleasure of meeting Jimmy Merchant. He is a very nice gentleman who signed a few posters and pictures for me when I was 16 years old. I am now 34 and still have those treasured items to this day. When we talked on my birthday in 2022, it truly made my day extra special. I consider Jimmy my friend and thank him for his friendship. Jimmy Merchant, you are, indeed, a legend!

Erin McCarthy

♫ ♫ ♫ ♫ ♫

I met Jimmy Merchant in 1973. I have always considered him a caring individual and simply just an overall good guy. I recall the days when I harmonized with Jimmy and a couple of other guys. Jimmy had an impeccable ear for harmony and arranging harmony parts. I used to like it when he came to my apartment, as he was well-liked by everyone in the old neighborhood and brought with him a contagious laugh that would get everyone going. We had great times over the years. They were full of fun and, of course, hard times as well. I always found Jimmy to be a straight-shooter and very positive. I remember when Jimmy was putting the group back together again in 1982. He contacted Herman Santiago, an original member of The

Teenagers, and off they went, traveling across the country and keeping the name of Frankie Lymon and The Teenagers alive. Without reservation, I must say that Jimmy was the driving force behind the group. He kept everyone in line and expertly managed them. Jimmy has a calm personality, but never mistake his kindness for weakness: Jimmy will correct you immediately, especially when it comes to music. I am honored to be Jimmy Merchant's friend and grateful for the countless times he has cheered me up.

Eddy Rezzonico

♫ ♫ ♫ ♫ ♫

I am Donald A. DaCosta, CEO of CrossRoads Entertainment LV, in partnership with Source 3 Entertainment and S3E Record Label, and owner of the "Inside the Music" television program. I have known Jimmy Merchant for some time and have worked closely with him. I'm pleased to say I consider him a "big brother." Throughout the years, he has been an inspiration to me, an invaluable source of information. He has helped me educate younger artists on how to navigate and avoid the pitfalls of the entertainment business. His words have been full of wisdom and inspiration to people needing his leadership and knowledge. From personal experience, he has been beyond helpful with his guidance regarding my business dealings, and his words of encouragement that accompany it have a solid religious foundation. Jimmy has been a shoulder to lean on in controversial and troubled times, and he is appreciated by other artists and friends who surround me. I truly value my relationship and friendship with Jimmy Merchant.

Donald A. DaCosta

♫ ♫ ♫ ♫ ♫

When most people with knowledge of American music history hear the name Jimmy Merchant, they immediately think of both the singing group he co-founded as a young teenager and their first hit song, which he wrote from a love letter given to him. That group became "Frankie Lymon and The Teenagers" and the song, *Why Do Fools Fall in Love*. That song was the first to skyrocket simultaneously up both the Pop and R&B charts. Jimmy also wrote many other of the group's musical hits but was not credited for doing so. Within weeks of his group's stardom, hundreds of copycat groups adopted their new sound, changing Rock 'n Roll from music written by and for adults to music written by and for kids. Frankie Lymon and The Teenagers immediately became global entertainment stars, were featured in two Rock 'n Roll movies, received stars on the Hollywood Walk of Fame, and were inducted into the Rock and Roll Hall of Fame. Not only were they the pioneers whose music climbed the Black and White music charts simultaneously, but their concerts in places like New York City's Paramount Theatre were the first where the kids tore down the demarcation barriers between Blacks and Whites — truly a beginning of a change in society, all because of music. Although the group's original history lasted only a few years, as the record company split the group in two, their history and music live on today. In those days, the music business was corrupt and abusive. Many songwriters and groups did not receive the rights and royalties for the music they wrote. Disappointingly, The Teenagers fall into that category. After being the top entertainment ticket in the world, the sky fell in on them. They went from the top of the world as young kids to falling into challenging and dark times. You will read how Jimmy spent many years in those dark years before renewing his faith in God, meeting his lovely wife, Mary, and living his life according to God's plan. Without hesitation, he gives solace to those in need and preaches God's Word to all who will listen. I have worked with him several times as he gave his time and talent to senior groups, church groups, and the physically and mentally challenged.

Truly, Jimmy Merchant has gone from extreme high points to extreme low points in life, but he has overcome those obstacles and become one of God's chosen to be about his Father's business.

Bob "Stretch" Kline

♫ ♫ ♫ ♫ ♫

I met Mr. Jimmy Merchant on Facebook in January 2017. Although we've never met in person, we became close through my interactions with his social media posts and conversations on Messenger. I must say that I've never felt closer to Mr. Merchant than as if he were my own flesh and blood — like that of a big brother living in another state. Initially, I didn't know he was a member of a singing group; I just liked a lot of his posts about God and his testimonies regarding the many blessings he has received. Then, as I looked much closer, I discovered his most beautiful talent as a singer with the legendary group, Frankie Lymon and The Teenagers. Learning that about him never changed my way of thinking toward him. To me, Mr. Merchant was just another person I met on Facebook at the time. To this day, his many posts continue to inspire me, as they have helped to shape me into a better person within my spirit and in my family. I truly believe Mr. Merchant is a beautiful soul sent to me by God to make a difference in my life. From what I can see, he's a caring husband and father, an honest, family-oriented man, and a God-fearing Christian. May God bless Mr. Merchant's book(s) and all he does in life.

Annice Cole

FOREWORD

My name is Mary Merchant. The year was 1956. I was 12 years old, living on West 112th Street in Harlem, when I first heard *Why Do Fools Fall in Love* by Frankie Lymon and The Teenagers on the radio. I recall falling in love with that song **instantly**. When the opportunity came to see The Teenagers at the famous Apollo Theater, I was amazed when I saw that group of five cute boys. As a teen girl, I never thought about which one was the cutest because, to me, they were **ALL** cute! Unlike the other adult performers on the stage that night, The Teenagers were singing and dancing, just for us teens. As they performed, they wore their signature white sweaters with a red capital 'T' on the front, and their very presence commanded the stage.

The Teenagers were role models for the rest of us, to the point that other teens began forming singing groups all over Harlem and the five boroughs of New York City: Manhattan, Brooklyn, Queens, The Bronx, and Staten Island. Four of my girlfriends and I formed a singing group, too. We had fun, but our "performances" went no further than rehearsals in my friend's apartment.

Every record that Frankie Lymon and The Teenagers made during the group's tenure was truly sensational. I remember how heartbroken my friends and I were when we learned Frankie had left the group. In fact, many fans—girls and boys alike—were very saddened because those five talented boys were no longer singing.

Fast forward a few years…

At age 18, I was introduced to jazz music. I had stopped listening to Doo-Wop (the style of music attributed to The Teenagers) and grew to love Motown and '70s R&B artists, especially Marvin Gaye. Doo-Wop was an exciting part of my *past*, and I left it there…or so I thought.

In 1991, I attended Christian Life Center on Linden Boulevard in Brooklyn, New York. One Sunday, a man approached me and asked, "What's your name? My name is Jimmy."

"My name is Mary," I replied.

"Mary is a beautiful name," he complimented.

I was flattered! Not once had I heard that smooth line before. Come to think of it, I had never received a single compliment about my name until Jimmy said it was *"beautiful."* I liked Jimmy instantly. He was handsome, very well-dressed, very soft-spoken, very polite, and even held a position in the church. After that day, every time I went to church, I saw Jimmy. After service, we had interesting conversations, which eventually led to us exchanging phone numbers. Every time we spoke, Jimmy talked about Jesus, read scriptures to me, and prayed with me (something I had **never** experienced with any other man). We actually had Bible study on the phone for a year in addition to learning more about each other's lives.

I remember the time, in July 1991, when Jimmy and I spent time together at our church's cookout in Connecticut. When we separated to socialize with other church members, I had a conversation with my friend Wanda. "I see you have a relationship with Brother Jimmy," she mentioned casually.

"Yes," I replied.

"Brother Jimmy is a very nice man," Wanda stated.

"I agree."

"Isn't it great that he's a Teenager?" she asked.

"A WHAT?" I replied incredulously. **"A TEENAGER?** Oh, no! I'm divorcing a man who acts like a teenager!"

"Oh, no! No! I don't mean **THAT** type of teenager. I mean that Jimmy Merchant is an original member of Frankie Lymon and The Teenagers!" Wanda said with a laugh.

At the time, I couldn't appreciate what Wanda said about Jimmy because I was thinking, **"Why didn't he tell me that?"** Needless to say, what should have been excitement at that moment was lost on me. Later, when I saw Jimmy again, the first thing I asked was, "Why didn't you tell me you are an original member of Frankie Lymon and The Teenagers?!"

His response blew me away and provided much-needed relief. "I wanted to learn about you, and I wanted to protect your heart. I didn't want you to know me as a performer. I want you to like me as a Christian man. I'm not perfect. God is still working on me."

We continued to talk over the phone, and a year later, we started dating. We admitted that we loved each other, so when Jimmy asked me to marry him, I said yes! We got married in June 1993. We will be married for an amazing 30 years in June 2023.

When Jimmy performed on stage, he became a Teenager all over again—and I was his biggest fan. He was no longer my husband when he was on that stage; he was Jimmy Merchant of The Teenagers. I loved seeing him perform! My admittedly biased **adult** opinion is that he was the *BEST* out of the whole group. He introduced me to show business, the backstage experience, the rehearsals, and his singing peers—and I **LOVED** it! I will be forever excited about my memorable experiences with Jimmy as an entertainer.

Oh, my goodness! **I MARRIED A TEENAGER!**

I am Mary Merchant: Jimmy Merchant's wife, his best friend, his prayer partner, and his greatest fan **EVER**! I love Jimmy Merchant!

Following are the words from a note he gave me a few years ago, and he loves the fact that I read it daily:

"Dear Mary,

Concerning our marriage, I have no regrets. You taught me what marriage is all about. If it wasn't for you, regarding our marriage, I do not know where I would be today."

That's my Jimmy — a man of many words…a man who was and still is a perfect gentleman. I'm so glad, and I thank God for my wonderful husband who loves the Lord. *Thank you, Jimmy, for choosing* **me** *to be your wife.*

Jimmy Merchant

PROLOGUE

"WHY DO FOOLS FALL IN LOVE — take 18!"

♫ ♫ ♫ ♫ ♫

"Deh doom bop…deh-doom bop…deh-doom bop…deh-doo-doe…"

"Ooh wah ooh wah…ooh wah ooh wah…ooh wah ooh wah… Why do fools fall in love?"

"Why do birds sing so gay…and lovers await the break of day…why do they fall in love?"

"Why…does the rain…fall from up above? Why do fools…fall in love? Why do they fall in love?"

♫ ♫ ♫ ♫ ♫

"CUT! HOLD IT! C'MON, BOYS! STEP BACK! Jimmy! Your first tenor is strong enough. Give Joe and Herman more room to be heard — especially Herman. Sherman! Your bass voice towers like you, as it should. NOW, FRANKIE! LISTEN! I am not feeling what I know you can do. Push harder, okay?"

"GEORGE! Hold on. To me, this song is the best yet! We rehearsed with Richie seemingly forever and all this week

after school. But, instead of you telling our parents to have us here on a Saturday when we are fully rested, you had us come here yesterday — AFTER SCHOOL! Then, when we got here, we had to wait for other singing groups to finish recording before we started — AFTER 10:00 PM.! Now, it's after MIDNIGHT on Saturday...18 INCOMPLETE TAKES LATER! Please! How about something to eat, okay?" Frankie complained.

"FRANKIE! Enough already! That's the energy I need — in your MICROPHONE! Richie, send the Chinaman to Howard Johnson's in Times Square to get the boys some hot dogs. Then you and I can talk."

♫ ♫ ♫ ♫ ♫

That account documents the original recording of the song *Why Do Fools Fall in Love* that led to our group's iconic fame. The date was Saturday, December 3rd, 1955, around 12:05 a.m. Bell Sound — a small, shabby, busy independent recording studio located on West 46th Street in New York City — was where it all took place.

Although it is 66 years later (at the time of this writing), those magnanimous moments in my life are still present — not only because they stand "in time" as the beginning of the youth movement in music history to this day, but also because they are indelibly fixed in my mind as the iconic lifetime experience that began for me as a **"DREAM."** Never did I think I would be one of five boys who would turn music around from adults recording music for adults to teenagers making records for kids, thereby becoming the greatest vocal group phenomenon to enter the music industry since the invention of record players.

♫ ♫ ♫ ♫ ♫

I, along with Joe Negroni, Herman Santiago, Sherman Garnes, and, of course, Frankie Lymon (all sharing two microphones), stood in front of George Goldner — the "Founding Father" of the most memorable 1950s Doo Wop classics (aka "Golden Oldies") ever recorded. Seated in a backward-turned chair, cleanly-shaven, with smoothly combed straight black hair, George was 'dapper' in his expensive slacks, silk socks, and well-shined banana shoes. He had removed his leather blazer, exposing a fitted powder blue dress shirt that complemented his gold tie, with the initials "GG" embroidered just above its pocket. The street-talking, unruffled Jew assured us the work we had done was not wasted. In fact, we had already quickly recorded a beautiful, slow love song that I wrote titled *Please Be Mine*, which became the flipside of *Why Do Fools Fall in Love*.

As we gave George our undivided attention, he flashed his cool, winning smile and said, "You boys got a big hit song on your hands, and the 'take' for it is just before you. So, think in those terms. Then comes fame. Not before." As he rose from his chair, he alerted his sax-playing bandleader, Jimmy Wright, saying, "Make sure your sax solo fits their song, okay?" Although it was a serious moment, Jimmy's '40s razzamatazz, hip, jive-talk response redirected everyone's seriousness, causing the five of us boys to crack up with laughter. Sherman's deep voice seemed to resonate louder than the rest. Nonetheless, George's aim at that moment was to comfort us.

While eating our hot dogs, George was in the reel-to-reel cutting room behind a thick glass partition talking to Al Weintraub (the studio owner/engineer) and Richard Barrett (the lead singer of "The Valentines"), who discovered us singing acapella on a street corner. Richard was a fast-talking military-like dude with a thick broom mustache and perfectly waved hair that Black entertainers like Nat King Cole wore at the time. As we finished eating, George and Richard—with their ties loosened—rejoined us. "Richie," George ordered, "tell the boys about the changes needed to upgrade their song."

Because of my group-harmony ability, Richard directed his words to me. "Jimmy, like the slow love song you boys recorded tonight before twelve, and because your idea for "Fools" came from a love letter, you turned it into a slow love song as well. When we decided to turn "Fools" into an up-tempo song—which made the song shorter timewise—you also straightened that out by adding ooh-wahs after Sherman's bass opening. Then, suggesting to re-sing the song after the sax solo, you solved the song's timing problem."

"So, what needs upgrading, Richie?" I asked.

Mr. Goldner interrupted. "You did good, but the song gets repetitious after the bridge, where it should build up with some kind of **HOOK**."

Joe, our baritone singer who knew about making records, calmly explained to the rest of us, "A 'hook' is a catchy phrase in a song that is "remembered" because it stands out...and can also make a song a big hit record!"

At that moment in time, our group's song began to be fully developed with the aid of Richard and George, who then gave Frankie a friendly, authoritative stare while saying, "Frankie, it's time to kick ass! Excuse me. Kick butt! Aim high! With punch! All because what you are doing is demanding for someone to tell you **WHY**! Why in the hell do fools fall in love?! *WHY* is the actual point of this song! Got it?"

Staring back at George with a fixed expression, Frankie replied, "I got it, George. **TELL ME WHY** is the *HOOK*!"

With Jimmy Wright's band back in place, Joe, Sherman, Herman, and I at one mic, and Frankie at his, Al's voice rang out of the loudspeaker:

"WHY DO FOOLS FALL IN LOVE — take 19!"

♫ ♫ ♫ ♫ ♫

Take 19 (and the four that followed) finally went all the way through, but they did not come without George's constant fixing and hardcore pushing for something explosive to happen concerning the 'hook.' Meanwhile, Frankie's anxiety drew him (at age 13) to tears. Never one to hold back, he spoke out. "George, what **more** do you want?! When will we be **done**?!"

With as much gentleness as he could muster, George consoled Frankie by saying, "Listen. Up to this point, I have spared you — as the group's lead singer —

to become completely familiar with this great song by riding its medium beat with your background vocals. While you are a gifted singer, your heart and soul must now take over, which is why I am stretching you for all it's worth. This is a once-in-a-lifetime shot for you five boys!"

We listened attentively to the playbacks as final sound adjustments for the piano, guitar, drums, and upright bass were made. I then noticed our group's background vocals were too low. When I told Joe to say something, Sherman suggested asking for a third mic. Herman's idea was to speak directly to Richard, who heard our complaints from our microphone inside the sound room's loudspeaker. "Tone it down, boys! We know what we're doing in here," Richard stated authoritatively.

George shouted to Jimmy Wright, "Whale off a signature sax solo, Jimmy — like you always do on our Gee & Rama 78 records!" Then, to the sound engineer, he ordered, "Turn the group harmonies up some."

As we were served more tea and lemon, and while the band took a quick smoke break, Joe and I noticed George was dissatisfied with our group name, "The Premiers." Jimmy Wright (knowing that George wanted something catchy) said, "George, they're teenagers. Name them **'The Teenagers.'"**

George turned and gave Mr. Wright a pleasant smile as Al (who was behind the glass partition) spoke up. "Gentlemen, it is well after 1:30 a.m. Let's do it!"

♫ ♫ ♫ ♫ ♫

"WHY DO FOOLS FALL IN LOVE — take 24!"

By the middle of that take, George — as a Jewish gentleman — was so into it, he could hardly remain seated. Although he had no rhythm or singing ability whatsoever, he began to seemingly mimic black love song singers by snapping his fingers and swiveling his head...off-beat. With his eyes closed, he gestured his arms toward us in a floating motion as if he seemingly saw us as winged choir boys, especially when the **"TELL ME WHY"** hook began to be fully expressed by Frankie...with love. As for us four background singers, we were caught up like Frankie (in another world). With everything we had, we targeted the completion of *Why Do Fools Fall in Love*. We knew George was really feeling it when he said, "Man...this feels so damn good!"

Al then snapped, *"WHY DO FOOLS FALL IN LOVE — take 25!"*

By then, everyone was pretty much wiped out. George made it seem easy for us five boys by keeping himself stationed directly in front of us, standing his ground like General Patton. He was relentless in driving us forward from beginning to end. When he asked Richard about our background vocals, Richard replied, "Terrific!" Realizing that my opinion counted as well, George asked me, "And what about you, Jimmy?"

"Speechless, George. Our song has been truly improved," I said with all honesty. We all agreed that Frankie's 'Tell Me Why' hook had gained its needed punch.

Looking back, I see that George Goldner not only knew what he had, but he also knew what to do with what he had. Turning to Frankie, he said, "Listen carefully, Frankie. We are there. I only need one more take for good measure. Please know that in this two-minute-eighteen-second song, I got to hear in your voice a begging question never answered. Overall, this is about a new 'boy' vocal group sound that you, along with Sherman, Herman, Joe, and Jimmy — blowing and pumping strong harmony — will smash racial barriers while pioneering to the music world a never heard greatness by kids…by **TEENAGERS!**"

Al Weintraub's final words that unforgettable night (or rather morning before 2:00 a.m.) stamped into record history and my life, a vocal group phenomenon when he said, "Boys…or shall I say, *'THE TEENAGERS.'*"

"WHY DO FOOLS FALL IN LOVE — take 26!"

INTRODUCTION – 1985...30 YEARS LATER

That great December 1955 moment referenced in the Prologue was the start of my boyhood dream coming to pass at age 15 that went full-force as a result of my vocal group's phenomenal *Why Do Fools Fall in Love* hit song history. And now, as a music legend (at age 83), my life story became a must-tell even moreso.

At age 45, there was a critical 20-minute moment in time that occurred in my life in 1985 that I am led to highlight here to prayerfully bless you, the reader.

The moment I am referencing occurred while I was sipping on a Heineken beer in the first booth of Tropical Gardens (aka 'TGs')—a bar and grill in the Washington Heights section of Manhattan, NYC. At the time, I felt utterly lost and thought to myself, "Where in the hell am I? Why am I here?" I no longer felt good about the legendary pioneer performer I had become as an original member of the 1956-57 vocal group that had accomplished hit after hit greatness on USA R&B charts and in foreign countries. Neither did I feel all the pleasantries associated with *Why Do Fools Fall in Love* being England's first American #1 Hit Parade record, labeling us **"THE RAGE OF THE**

AGE." Although those achievements were primarily due to our song's rerouting of music toward kids — the very thing that fulfilled my musical kid dreams — at age 45, it all meant zero.

Interestingly, key incidentals were also meaningless, including the location of TGs being blocks away from the school where my kid group performed. Not far from there was a twirling light atop the George Washington Bridge that I stared at as a child from a Bronx window where I grew up, dreaming my grandiose dreams.

As I observed the rush-hour thoroughfare and dress wear of passersby that differed from the 1950s through TGs tinted front glass pane, my thoughts were on Nina, the woman of West Indian and Cuban descent who was the barmaid and my love interest at the time. She was very sensual, which kept my sexual needs attached to her — despite our topsy-turvy involvement and her strange, disoriented ways.

Despite being a cool, level-headed guy on the outside, on the inside, I constantly wondered, "Where in the hell am I headed now?" All of that was going on in and around me while serious concerns about my revitalized vocal group (with only one other original member) were once again at their end.

You see, 1950s Doo-Wop shows and vocal groups had become prevalent yet again during the early-80s. Therefore, there was money to be made. Herman Santiago (the other living group member) and I reformed. Although Herman had been inactive up to that point, it felt good just being back on stage. Sadly, as our group's leader, I could not hustle gigs due to not having a booking agent. Coupled with deep, personal issues with Nina, I found myself discouraged and sucked dry. My renewed life's dream was put on the back burner once again.

Yet another dilemma I faced was having to return to driving a NYC yellow taxi to make a living. It was a "problem" because the reality was it could potentially lead me back to being a dope addict that wrecked my life, marriage, and relationships with my six children. Yet, driving was the only other way I knew to earn money at the time. Although drug use was behind me, the ever-present age-old questions in my soul remained: "Who am I? Why was I born?" That dilemma seriously needed to be resolved.

As I continued sipping on my beer and keeping a watchful eye on Nina as she tended the bar with mostly just-paid employees from the nearby Presbyterian Hospital, my thoughts of my group's former fame bombarded my brain...and they were discouraging. Although the group had become "Superstars" before that term was coined, we were history by mid-1957. Blindly, our management team had overlooked our full potential with Frankie Lymon by making him a solo artist. While Frankie's sad death in 1968 was a loss to the music industry, it also ended all hope of our group ever rejoining. Then, as the other two original members passed away, my thoughts reverted to rising to fame as a solo artist. After all, that was **my dream**, right? Unfortunately, while it would have been a remarkable exception to the rule, it proved to be a big mistake.

Despite my discomfort with Nina, we would often end up at my apartment for overnight sexcapades—a significant trade-off that began at the age of 16 when I used my group's fame to cruise mainly White girls backstage while on tour in 1956-57 in the U.S. Some of the key theaters where we also pulled Black girls were: The Royal (Baltimore, MD), The Uptown (Philadelphia, PA), The State (Hartford, CT), The Howard (Washington, DC), The Fox (Detroit, MI), The Apollo (Harlem, NY), and at both Paramount Theaters in NYC with the infamous DJ, Alan Freed. Yes, we were five clean-cut and relatively innocent boys at first, but we were taught by older vocal group singers and musicians who were all about sex, drugs, and Rock 'n' Roll. It was no surprise to me that I remained stuck on sex in 1985 with an insatiable barmaid who used men to get back at one who had wronged her in some way.

So, there I was, staring motionless at my almost-completed beer while waiting for Nina to get off. Suddenly, Herman's advice came to mind: "Stick it out." While our return to the stage in 1981 was a breath of fresh air and raised goosebumps at the mere thought of re-establishing our presence on the music scene, Herman's overall inabilities were seemingly a burden due to being spacy.

While we street corner vocal groups from the mid-'50s basically imitated band instrumentation using "ooohs," "waaas," "doos," and "wopps," Herman and I (much like other group singers of our time) found our cool, unintellectual street music labeled "Doo-Wop" somewhat demeaning—but that label stuck to '50s groups and wasn't all bad. After all, we had returned not as five guys but as three sharp, good-looking background singers with a dazzling female Frankie Lymon sound-alike lead singer that our fans buzzed about: **"THEIR MAGIC IS BACK!"** What uplifted Herman and me was the phenomenal remake of *Why Do Fools Fall in Love* by Diana Ross, which became vital to a movie about our group and opened the possibility of us getting singers' royalties as the true subjects of "The Great American Royalty Rip-Off."

What is key for you — the reader — that I was led to reference here in the Introduction regarding those 20 minutes in the bar is the following incident...

As I sat in the front booth, looking out at the happenings on the other side of the glass window, I noticed a familiar face peering in. It was Clementine — a former girlfriend who worked at Presbyterian Hospital — and she unexpectedly came in. After she hugged a co-worker who was leaving, I politely greeted her. With a glow-like facial expression, Clementine replied, "Praise the Lord, Jimmy!"

After taking her to meet Nina, we sat in the booth and conversed. She began the conversation. "After we separated, I became a born-again, saved Christian." When I asked her about being 'saved,' she answered, "It is receiving by faith Jesus Christ and being saved from Hell. According to God, all things happen for a reason, not by coincidence. See, I normally cash my paycheck to the right of TGs at lunchtime, but I needed vegetables from the store to the left for Thanksgiving, so I decided to wait and cash my check after work. Then, as I glanced through TGs window, there you were!" She then briefly closed with, "Listen, Jimmy. I believe God wants your undivided attention, so I will be praying for your salvation." After inviting me to her house for Thanksgiving, just as quickly as she appeared, she disappeared from TGs.

Curious thoughts drew my mind to a living room scene where my two grandmothers once lived above Harlem. I recalled my time as a youngster with my two sisters when I observed women with warm facial expressions (much like Clementine's) encircling my great-grandmother, praying. She then turned to look at me (much like Clementine did) and, seeing something special in my sisters and me, said, "Children, the main thing God wants for everyone is **SALVATION**. Now, let us pray."

My sepia-colored thoughts were then interrupted by Nina. "I can tell you want to see that woman again, don't you?"

I politely replied, "No. I need **money**, not somebody's *church*. It's after five. Let's get out of here." While scooting along from TGs in my customized black van, on the hunt for cocaine and marijuana for Nina and me, I wondered about those "40 years apart" scenarios as mentioned in the Holy

Bible. I thought about not having a single idea where I was in life, and although I had an uplifting return to music in 1981, my great American dream was gone again. I had no choice but to return to driving a cab — an adventure that was sure to lead me back to a life of crime, jail, or an overdose of heroin (an experience I had previously experienced).

As we rode down Amsterdam Avenue, passing where my grandmothers lived, I recalled my great-grandmother's main two words while praying: "**SALVATION** and **ETERNITY**."

TABLE OF CONTENTS

A Teenager's Dream

CHAPTER 1: HARLEM

Dreams. We all have them. The realization of them, however, is often hit-or-miss. As for me, I was one of four 9th-grade boys whose vocal group added a younger kid to sing lead and became world-renowned in 1956 after our first hit song hit the air. The musical gifts that led to my singing dreams truly stand out in my mind. Also, while those experiences while growing up prepared me to be one of the beginners in America's youth movement in music, there are family factors that were in place before my parents, James Rubin Merchant and Elsie Jane Mosby, met in Harlem, fell in love, and got married. And, while Harlem happens to be in Manhattan (one of the five boroughs of NYC, from 110th to 155th Streets), it, too, has dream scenarios that, in fact, aided and fed my musical dream.

In talking with my dear, darling mom earlier in life, she shared that she and my dad formally met in 1936 when she was 16 and he was 19 years old. She loved art (a certain quality of my life derived from her) and, coincidently, graduated from Stitt Junior High School in 1935—the same school just above Harlem where my group formed and four of us graduated from. Then, desiring to be a secretary, she attended Central Commercial High School in Downtown

Manhattan. It was at that time she noticed my father checking her out in her Harlem neighborhood.

One afternoon, when turning the corner of 119th Street and 8th Avenue on the way to the grocery store for her mother, she observed my father watching her again from the other side of the avenue as he and his buddy Chucky rode their bicycles. "They stopped, and he then whistled," she stated. That whistle, where he used a finger from each hand at the tip of his tongue to get someone's attention from a distance, later became familiar to my two sisters and me, which was just one of the special things about him. My mother then added, "That special whistle basically told me there was something special about me that always caught his undivided attention." My mom was a darling-looking female, and I seemed to have inherited my father's eye for beauty. She then added, "It was his friend who gave him the confidence to introduce himself and politely ask if I might go bike riding with him. He offered to teach me when I told him I didn't know how." After sharing that she was a shy girl, she concluded with, "While seeing your father as a sharp guy, and your grandmother allowing him to take me on a double-decker bus to the movies on 42nd street along with some other young ladies, I learned he loved jazz."

That, dear reader, was where my musical dreams were initiated, followed by my mother's love for male love song singers. Regarding my powerful "dream factor," I later learned that well before my parents met, Harlem had not only become an extraordinarily remarkable location as the Black Capital of America, but it was also a multi-crossroads of ideas and dreams.

From a musical perspective, a significant aspect of Harlem's Black idiom that got my dad's attention when he arrived there from the south was its Black music movement, which aided enormously as it related to my life's dream factor. In my youth, I learned that the rhythm of jubilee, gospel, and blues (all sounds born on farms and fields in the south) was where the Black music movement came about, called Rock 'n' Roll. As I watched my parents dance to jazz, swing, and bebop music, my entertainment dreams were also fed.

I feel it is important to note the following: Before the 1960s Motown era, Soulful sounds of the '70s, and Rap of the '80s Hip-Hop culture, the mid-1950s brought into existence street corner acapella singing vocal groups—a movement that was birthed in Harlem and other locations dubbed "Doo-Wop."

Now, regarding the "beforehand" family dream factors referenced... Upon researching their history, three instances stand out more than any others.

The first is with my great-grandfather, George Merchant. He was a seaman from Barbados who got married in the British West Indies to a woman named Lulia. Desiring to spend more time with his family, he gave up being a seaman to work inland after the birth of their third child. In 1908, he followed his dream and migrated to America with his family, where they settled in Sumter, South Carolina. My father was born there to Gertrude, my great-grandfather's eldest daughter.

The other two very explosive dream factors that aid my life's story strongly concern my parents' mothers. Although the two women never met (because one died before their two children met), not only were they both named Gertrude, but they also had the same dream: to relocate to none other than Harlem, NY, in 1925.

Black families were pouring into Harlem en masse from rural southern homelands and the West Indies for better living conditions and work wages never before even dreamed of. Gertrude Merchant (my dad's mother) and Gertrude (Carter) Mosby (my mom's mother) both did just that after failed marriages...and both had one child each. They relocated from Sumter, NC, and Philadelphia, PA, respectively, after learning about the great migration and mass movement of Blacks to the urban north.

Of notable importance is that after two negative relationship events, my father's mother was encouraged to take her father's advice and pursue her NYC dream, which she did. Her first relationship had ended at the age of 17 (that was with my grandfather). She then married a Greek gentleman who owned a candy establishment my father loved as a child, but she left him after a drunken abuse incident.

Interestingly, although she never married my grandfather, she gave my father his last name: Merchant. When her mom died, she placed my dad (at age eight) with her Sumter, SC family, promising to send for him once she settled in Harlem with her brother George, Jr., and sister Jeanette. Later, due to a severe illness in Harlem Hospital and feeling sorry about not seeing her son (my father) for ten years, my aunt Jeanette (who became a nurse and worked in the hospital) sent for my father to see his mom. Sadly, she passed away in my aunt's arms before he arrived, simply because she failed to include the address of Harlem Hospital in her hurry to send him a telegram — and even after consulting with a policeman who directed him to the elevated train to Harlem.

While my father (also called 'Sammy') was upset about not seeing his mother before she passed, my aunt Jeanette shared, "He had already become very street savvy and mature growing up to age 18 in the south." He then moved in with her family and began shining shoes on the NYC streets using a homemade portable shoebox to earn his way until acquiring a job shining shoes in a Harlem barbershop.

Regarding my mother's backstory: She was born on November 4, 1920. At age five, she came to Harlem with her mother. While her father (Edward Mosby) was sadly an unfaithful husband to her mother, she shared with me that he was a suave Philly gentleman who loved and adored her to no end, even going so far as to take her to his job in her carriage to "show her off." My mom added that although her mother had decided to leave her father (which hurt her deeply), her mother's overall aim — or "dream" (like that of my father's mom) — was to relocate to Harlem with him, she did so immediately after another woman poisoned him. One of 11 children, my mother's mom was dedicated to her entire family but mainly to her mother, Martha Jane Carter, who, when she left for Harlem with my mother, took her own mother as well.

My great-grandmother was incredibly special. She was the first-born and the highly regarded matriarch of her huge Philadelphia Carter family. At 22, she became a born-again Christian and closely served God as a stewardess and usher in a Philly church. She did the same when she arrived in Harlem while attending the highly honored Mother A.M.E. Zion Church.

Thinking back to my days as a youngster, I recall noticing her talking to someone that no one else saw with deep love, whether standing or on her knees. That person, of course, was God. Other times, she would single me out while praying with other women and whisper various things like, "James, close your eyes"—even though my attention was sometimes sidetracked by other things, like the floor model record machine with records stacked on it.

What inadvertently enters my dream thoughts is something my mother said when I told her about writing this book: "As you later learned in life, Jimmy, along with gospel music being about the Lord, your musical dream influences started on both sides of your family." She went on to explain. "As a little girl, when your great-great-grandmother had to take care of me while my mother worked, although she was a woman of God, she worked mainly at musical locations, joyfully talking about them. My mom first began as a cashier booth worker in a downtown NYC theater and then in Harlem at the Lafayette Theatre—a key entertainment establishment that led to other top Black show spots in Harlem, such as the Savoy and Renaissance Ballrooms, where Black performers including Louis Armstrong and Lena Horne sang," she stated with evident pride.

My grandmother later told me that along with working as a cashier at the Savoy Ballroom—a club known as one of the first racially-integrated venues in the country known as the "Home of Happy Feet" that brought Black shows and performers in from 1926 to 1958—she also worked at Harlem's Smalls Paradise. That establishment was owned by Tommy Smalls, also known as Dr. Jive on WWRL Black radio (a gentleman I later met). Before working in a nursing home security office, that was her longest music job.

Before I conclude this chapter, I want to give you a brief overview of my mom's life up to the time she married my father.

Her mother was strict and firm with her and her look-alike first cousin Martha, who moved in with them. They were two light-skinned teen beauties with long hair, unable to do much of anything unless it was for special events. They had little freedom. "Even while chased after by a lot of young guys," my mom once said. After explaining about my father and then becoming pregnant, that relationship was allowed, enabling them to rent their own place before marrying in 1938. The following year, she gave birth to a baby girl in Harlem Hospital, whom she named Gertrude Elsie (after her mother and herself). Then, when she was about to give birth to me 11 months later in 1940, with Harlem Hospital being crowded, they sent her to one in another NYC borough known as The Bronx. A year later, in 1941, my sister Jean Ruth Ann came, prompting my parents to find a larger apartment immediately. Amazingly, my dad politely refused when my grandmother (who still resided in Harlem with my great-grandmother) offered my parents two of her rooms. Interestingly, that location — 512 West 156th Street in Manhattan, just a block above Harlem in an area called Washington Heights — later played a key role regarding my dream factor.

When my father located a larger apartment in Harlem, my mother shared with me that while she also wanted them away from Harlem, due to my father being a busy poker card-playing gambler there, she politely said no. Then, my mother wisely found a neighborhood across the East River Bridge between Harlem and The Bronx. When she took him to see the nice five-room fourth-floor apartment, they both liked it and chose to make that our new home.

Fun Fact: "Morrisania" is the name of the section of The Bronx where we lived and the name of the hospital where I was born on February 10, 1940, at 2:35 a.m. due to Harlem Hospital having no room for new births.

CHAPTER 2: THE BRONX

The historic music part of my life began in the Bronx at age 14 when my parents relocated from Harlem with my two sisters and me. I often spent time staring in wonder at that outside world from the 4th-floor window of my parents' bedroom when they were out, never knowing what was in store for me. The back windows of our apartment looked out over a children's playground that my sisters and I played in, but the front view was the one that most often held my attention. The five-story building was located on the first block of Boston Road, angling off the thoroughfare known as Third Avenue. Both roads were made of rugged cobblestone. Along with the trolly streetcars that rolled on the tracks below our window, I mused at the dynamics of the uptown-downtown elevated subway trains anchored above the Third Avenue street traffic. As the roar of the trollies and 'L' trains traveled their usual routes, my curious, youthful eyes were calmed by peacefully flying homing pigeons being trained on a rooftop just across the two thoroughfares.

Before my mom would send me to bed at night, I stared at a twirling stage-like searchlight atop the George Washington Bridge. At nightfall, apart from viewing the moon, I gazed at a celestial star formation that favored a sequined curtain. The interesting point here is that I had not the faintest clue that the Washington Heights section of Manhattan, where my grandmother and great-grandmother lived, was the very area where my "dream to sing," followed by fame, was to begin.

While I miss and love my mother dearly and all that she shared with me, the second thought that comes to mind in the Bronx regarding 'my dream' is my dad, who unknowingly aided the dream to surface when he returned from the Army in 1946. Although he was a mature, classy, sharp, cool cat who took on the responsibility of raising my two sisters and me after marrying our mother, I'm choosing to share with you the critical role he played at the start of my life regarding my ultimate dream.

For those who can remember, the color-line barrier was broken by baseball player Jackie Robinson in 1947. That strengthened my dad's love for baseball and the New York Yankees. His desire was for me to become a baseball player as well, even though his specialty was his love for Jazz and Bee-Bop. Those sounds opened my musical gifts in preparation for Doo-Wop. My father held my undivided attention before age six and throughout my early school years as it related to music when I observed him listening to and imitating instruments. As he puffed on a Camel cigarette, I carefully watched him take a full-size jazz record from its box, open the floor model record player that my mom purchased when he was in the Army, place the vinyl disk onto the turntable under the record player's arm, and then slide the switch to the 'on' position. I marveled at how the big-band sound moved my father. Before I knew it, I was off and running, grasping into my soul (without truly understanding) the slick orchestrations of songs like "Little Girl Blue" by Duke Ellington. In fact, arrangements like those that used smooth-sounding various instruments soothed my musically-gifted 'hearing ears.' Additionally, while watching my father imitate the intricate soloing of horn players like Charley "Yard Bird O' Rooney" Parker and Dizzy Gillespie doing their 1945 up-tempo intricate version of "Koko" on Savoy Records, the dawning of my dream to sing was unknowingly born.

Before the age of six, my two sisters and I didn't really know our father. That was primarily due to two "situations": 1. My mom getting him inducted into the Army after World War II in order to pay bills with his allotment checks, and 2. Him not being home because he was a non-working Harlem gambler. Despite his weakness but wanting to show us love while in the

Army, he sent my sisters and me tiny three-minute records with a loving fatherly voice made in an arcade booth. While that was great, his love for music and records held my attention the most. Then, of course, my imagination went into overdrive when he returned from the Army, and I got to know him better.

I'll never forget that January 1946 day when our doorbell rang, and my mom told me to buzz the person in. At first, after looking four floors down and seeing a man coming up the flights of steps with a heavy green cloth bag over his shoulder, I thought he was a laundry guy. When he looked up at me in his soldier's outfit while turning to the last stairway, my mom alerted me, saying, "That's your daddy!"

Before removing his coat, he hugged and kissed my two sisters. To me, he said, "Hi, son." Those two words were special to me, but what made the moment even more spectacular was seeing a cool, sophisticated cat whom I hoped to one day emulate like most sons think and do. Seeing that desire in me, he took me to see the movie "Red River" two years later when he learned I favored cowboys like Roy Rogers. Starring John Wayne, the movie was about a cattle baron/rancher who fights with his foster son (actor Montgomery Clift), which was far more real than Roy

Rogers and Gabby Hayes! He called it "a real cowboy movie."

Despite my father's cool personality and seemingly good potential working in the so-called gambling trade, it took me a while to learn that his overall behavior as a family man would fail. Initially, he took my mom's advice and used his GI Bill money for cooking school. Then, he went to tailoring school while pressing clothes part-time. When those efforts did not work for him, he returned to the streets of Harlem, hustling as a number runner and poker-playing gambler.

Through all that my mom experienced with my father before and after the Army, I cannot put into words the great wife she was to him. Along with working various jobs, she aided him on summer weekends when he needed her as his cute cook while having all-night card gambling sessions in our home. Our mother even went so far as to have her mother and grandmother care for my sisters and me during our elementary school breaks so that she could look out for him. While with our grandmothers, they took us to Yankee Stadium to hear preaching by Billy Graham. He taught about being saved from Hell by becoming a born-again Christian and salvation. We also frequented the well-known Mother A.M.E. Zion

Church that grew during the Harlem Renaissance —
the place where Black Americans from southern states
and the Caribbean flocked to, just as the mothers of
both my parents did.

Regarding my music dreams, what comes to
mind when at my grandmother's was when my great-
grandmother prayed with her small group of women.
While there with my two cute sisters, she always tried
to keep my undivided attention on Jesus. Yet, as I
patted her dog, Rex, my eyes were focused on the
Zenith floor-model radio and phonograph Victrola
record player and the great picture on the wall above
it of my Uncle Francis. That photo, just like his true
self, showed a smooth, sharp-looking, dark-skinned,
elegant cabaret musician who was both an organist
and entertainer with his duo piano-playing buddy.
They were known as Carter and Bowie. My uncle's
clean-cut, well-groomed, classic stage style, smelling
of a nice cologne with a suave haircut under his
occasional derby, wearing a classy double-breasted
suit with matching handkerchief and bowtie, held my
attention when he visited. He gave me a close-up view
of what being a suave stage personality was all about.

I had no idea that the specific photo of him and
Mr. Bowie that NYC photographer James J. Kriegsman
took would later be used for my group when we

became stars. Neither did I ever think that having to relocate to Los Angeles with his wife and daughter, he would grant me a gift: his Baby Grand piano. I was blown away by incidents like those, as each proved to benefit my musical dreams.

At age nine, while maturing as a quiet boy and becoming even more observant, my mom began taking my sisters and me to the church around the corner from us on 164th Street. Grace Gospel Church was established in 1922 and is still standing there today. During the time that we attended services, Dr. Bente was the pastor. Grace Gospel kept us busy. We attended Bible classes to learn about Jesus, went on outings to Tibbets Brook Park, and visited Jones Beach during the summer, where we enjoyed fun and games. They also organized a Boy Scout group, Troop 100, and two basketball teams for elementary and high school boys.

Outside of church, I was the only male at home besides my militant, disciplinarian father. While looking at me, he repeatedly said, "I am the boss of this house, and you will follow my orders!" That was said as my sisters assisted our mother with kitchen work and swept the floors. I was tasked with mopping, packing laundry, cleaning the bathroom, and shining both his and my shoes using his old shoeshine box. Whenever I failed or missed out on a task, I was put on punishment and could not go outside with my buddies. I also assisted my sister Gert with keeping an eye on our sister Jean while on the playground. Our dad, who watched us from our kitchen window (when he was home), would whistle to get our attention using the same whistle first used to get our mom's attention. Both entrances to the park where I played marbles, jumped the fence from swings, and hung out with my buddies were on the side streets of our block: Teasdale and 164th Street, across from our church.

At age ten, some good news came my way. My father began giving me an allowance of $1.00 a week. That money enabled me to get away with my buddies on Saturdays and go to the movie theater on Boston Road to The Tower. At the time, shows were a mere ten cents. During those adventures, exposure to "SHOW BUSINESS" was gained. Some influences included Looney Tunes, Universal International, 20th Century Fox, and MGM musicals. The prominent list of actors and actresses I saw on the big screen was vast. Still, some of the more memorable include Roy Rogers and his wife Dale Evans, Alan Ladd, Tony Curtis, Rita Heyward, Hedy Lamar, Liz Taylor, and Marilyn Monroe. The list of singers included Judy Garland, Doris Day, and Esther Williams.

My young eyes were also drawn to great dancers such as Fred Astaire and Gene Kelly, as well as jokesters Abbott & Costello and bad guys like James Cagney, Orson Wells, and Lon Chaney (who was no joke as "The Wolfman"). I cannot fail to mention the Black singers such as Paul Leroy Robeson, Louis Armstrong, Billie Holiday, Bessie Smith (whom I saw sing and act in the 1925 Black 15-minute short film, "St. Louis Blues"), and Lena Horne (who I later lived near while in Brooklyn, NY).

Fun Fact: The premier Black actor, Sidney Poitier (who was from the Bahamas), served in the Army with my dad and later played cards with him as well.

Despite being moved by movie heroes like Superman, Tarzan, Zorro, and Batman, to copying drawings of them from comic books, show business and music entertainment became an unwavering desire—especially vocal group singing. In fact, while watching a movie one Saturday at The Tower, a short news clip of four White guys singing smooth harmony like my dad's jazz records blew me away! The Four Freshmen vocal group was discovered in 1948 by band leader Stan Kenton. The group's style was modeled after Stan's trombone instrument sound. Two of their many excellent songs are "I Remember You" and

"Day by Day," but when I heard their opening of "It's a Blue World" and how they used their voices in the jazz tradition, I was stunned by what came to be known as something called acapella. Acapella expresses a song's lyrics with warm feelings without instruments. They also accompanied themselves using 'blow harmony' tones like 'oohs and waahs' in place of horns. My abilities to hear individual harmony parts were further intrigued.

Another group I saw in a clip called "Official Films" who did more of the same and then some was the phenomenal, undervalued, supremely skilled pioneer Black vocal group, The Mills Brothers, who first sang in church. After their audition in 1929, they were put on the radio immediately. Singing with a home-grown classic, unique style (initially taught to them by their parents), they emulated the tonality of brass instruments, including a tuba. They also imitated violins, violas, and a string base as one member imitated a harmonica. Their father joined the group when one of them passed away, but overall, they took vocal group singing to another place with songs like "Up a Lazy River." Coincidentally, while singing the song "Paper Doll," out of the clear blue, one stated the words 'Doo-Wop'—an indication that Black American jazz and the mid-'50s Black vocal group movement had an influence on them after the Rock 'n' Roll explosion on the radio.

Better yet (still at age ten), while learning of those two groups that sharpened my harmony ability, along with others like "The Pied Pipers" with Jo Stafford singing "Dream," I saw an awe-inspiring Black vocal group in another short music entertainment film clip at the Tower Theatre. They were fun yet sophisticated with a groovy show style, smoothly drawing women to them while performing their Harlem hit song, "Take the 'A' Train." That moment took me somewhere else! As they further enhanced my singing dreams, I imagined being ON STAGE! Of course, it was just a dream, but it began to feel attainable.

After experiencing that short scene, that smooth group of Black dudes debuted in 1934 and became known as The Delta Rhythm Boys. While on stage, those four were cool-singing Black actors. In fact, they smoothly presented themselves while moving forward with a zealous, joyful street atmosphere toward 'Sugar Hill'...way up in Harlem via the A-train subway. While singing "Take the 'A' Train" (in the context of attracting beautiful, swing-dancing Black women around them), what also stood out to me, along with their groovy harmonies, was their slick instrument imitations.

Also, at that time, I learned of another Black team of older gentlemen who made international fame before I was born: the great Ink Spots with their hit song "I Don't Want to Set the World on Fire." They had laid-back vocals behind their convincing lead singer, which their suave-speaking bass singer backed. The group's unique four-part harmony is what truly made them superstars.

I cannot leave out yet another very influential group of Black gentlemen from Baltimore, also out in 1948, that opened my dreams all the more, especially when I later got to see them perform live. What's important here is while I did not see them on the big screen, I first heard them on the radio. They were called Sonny Til and The Orioles. They, too, took vocal group singing to higher heights with their very popular love song, "It's Too Soon to Know." The group was first heard live on the Arthur Godfrey Sunday Radio Talent Show. My buddies and I freaked out as we copied their singing style! Although the listeners strongly loved their romantic singing style, they lost that contest. However, they were chosen to remain on Arthur's weekly show nonetheless. I believe that decision was made because they mainly attracted the listening ears and attention of the female audience.

Interestingly, a few years later, when appearing live, their sexy slow song lead singer caused gangs of girls to run up to the stage for hugs (this was before Elvis Presley or The Beatles received that kind of attention internationally). I was over-the-top impressed by all that I heard from the group on the radio, the attention they received from girls, and how the girls allowed boys to slow dance with them at length. THE STAGE began to exercise its irrefutable tug on me.

While those 'ON STAGE' thoughts were enhanced as I moved into age 11 (1951), something else occurred that I must briefly inject regarding my dad's life when he became a working man in Harlem. He had, in fact, begun working at two Harlem bowling alleys just off 125th Street as a pin-boy, setting up pins for bowlers. He sometimes took me with him to watch him work. Soon after, he surprisingly became a top-flight professional bowler, acquiring fame as the first Black man to bowl three perfect games in a row. It was no small feat to bowl a '300' (all strikes) in one game, let alone three in a row! Before going to bowling tournaments in places like Detroit, MI, where my mom also went to see him, he had her bring my sisters and me to watch him bowl in the Bronx. There was a photo of my father presented in Ebony Magazine where he was bowling at one of the Harlem locations on 125th Street, but the famous Apollo Theatre stood out to me most at that moment. It was in that place where a wave of R&B vocal groups would be seen with an explosion of love songs first heard on radio airwaves and 78 records, purchased primarily by vocal group lovers. I cannot leave out the oncoming hordes of females excited about their front-row seat tickets to see groups like The Orioles in person—ON STAGE—singing their slow, sexy love songs at the APOLLO, where they got live hugs.

Along with great love song-singing groups during that time were a few with bird-like names. They included:

- 1950—The Ravens, with their dramatic bass singer, Mr. Jimmy Ricks, singing their vintage classic "Count Every Star."
- 1951—The Larks on Apollo Records, singing "My Reverie."
- 1951—Eddie Rich and The Swallows with "Will You Be Mine," "Beside You," and "Eternally."
- 1953—The Flamingoes with an incredible love song titled "Golden Teardrops."

- 1953 — The Crows singing "Gee." ('Gee' became the title of the company my group later recorded with.)

Overall, each love song contained elements of Doo-Wop.

A vital love song fact that I later learned is that they override other released song types and are often far more successful. Basically, when one thinks about writing a song, "love" is usually the concept — whether it be about happiness, breaking up, or making up. The same applies to songs written about a female when her name is used as the song's title, many of which both vocal groups and solo singers sang. A few examples sung by groups are:

- "Florence" by The Paragons
- "Valerie" by The Starlites
- "Denise" by Randy and The Rainbows
- "Barbara Ann" by The Regents
- "Blanche" by The 3 Friends

Another with a stand-out 1-6-2-5 base and chord movement with piano triplets that later became the Doo-Wop vocal group trademark that all potential '50s groups coined was "Nadine," released in 1953 by The Coronets. Then, there is "Gloria," released in 1954 by The Cadillacs (my vocal group met their lead singer, Speedo, at a Harlem JHS talent show just before our fame and worked with him afterward).

Unknowingly, those things were being instilled in me to make my dream happen. Along with coming to realize the 'ON STAGE' part of a vocal group performing with class and presence while singing all types of love songs with a flavor that embraced listening females near and far, the real job was recording written songs to make hits. Significantly, the lead and backup singers were tasked with showing up ON STAGE convincingly, like each knew their job — with or without musical training, especially when recording. I was taking it all in like a sponge in an ocean. I couldn't get enough!

With that in mind, a particular lady drawn to solo love song singers like Frank Sinatra and Tony Bennett, whom I cannot fail to mention, is my dear, darling mother. The two she loved the most (and took my sisters and me to see) were Nat King Cole, singing "Unforgettable," and Mr. Billy Eckstine, performing "From the Bottom of My Heart," whose voice I copied as if I were ON STAGE (when we got back home, of course). Humorously, I mimicked his sex appeal, trying to get my mother's and sisters' attention — which I did.

Combining that fun experience with my mom and thoughts of my father when he arrived home from the Army, although their love for music differed slightly, they both aided my musical dream thoughts — albeit unbeknownst to them.

I remember watching my father smoothly dancing with my mom to Billie Holiday's music and then seeing him copy the showmanship of Cab Calloway on our living room floor alone. My kid eyes saw attention-getting, stage-like qualities to copy, such as how he used the soles of both shoes to slide back and forth like he was sanding the floor. When I asked, "Dad, what's the name of that dance?"

"The Sand," came his reply. Then, while doing 'The Sand,' he imitated jazz solo instruments with his voice rising above the background band music. When I asked about that, he said, "That's what they call 'scatting.' It's basically imitating a Be-Bop horn solo, like a free-style musical instrument, improvising during the middle of a song." Although my father never studied music, his ability to copy the Be-Bop sound with his voice caught my deep undivided attention.

The skilled trumpet player and entertainer Mr. Dizzy Gillespie headed Be-Bop. It was he who used a free-style counter phraseology that players like jazz saxophonist Charlie "Yardbird a 'Rooney" Parker (1920-1955) and Ella Fitzgerald joined with to do his thing. First, from the early '40s Swing to Rebop, then from Be-Bop to Bop, it was a name coined from 'nonsense syllables' by Dizzy Gillespie. Dizzy verbalized (or talked) like a musical instrument to be more entertaining. My father saw and copied that style.

Regarding "Be-Bop," I am reminded of how the '50s vocal group singing phrase "Doo-Wop" came to be. Like "Be-Bop," the term "Doo-Wop" began to be used in Black neighborhoods by vocal group background singers imitating horns they didn't have and couldn't afford.

Before moving on from elementary school, I was presented with an important certificate in January 1951 by my 5th-grade teacher, Mrs. Jacobs. It was a Service Certificate for "Efficient Service as a School Aide" that, incidentally, my great-grandmother truly loved as with everything about me. Before passing in her sleep at age 78 in February, she told me by phone, "James, we're called to serve, which takes time to learn." After my mother spoke to her during that same call, she turned and said, "I agree with grandma." I had not the slightest idea what 'to serve' meant.

Meanwhile, I was beginning to mature and get around on my own. I sometimes even took the crosstown 161st bus or trolly to run errands and walk Rex for my strict grandmother. While chewing her gum and smoking a Chesterfield cigarette, she would pleasantly hug me and then give me two dollars for a job well done. On my return trip home, I passed both the Polo Grounds (where the NY Giants played) and Yankee Stadium, thinking about the popularity of sports — mainly baseball that my father wanted me to get into. Then, when I encountered my first male teacher that September, I learned he was very strict…much like my father was on me in particular. I was attending an all-boys JHS with a reputation for fighting. That teacher's counsel was truly needed.

In February 1952, at age 12, the church Boy Scout Master, Mr. Charles Meriwether, asked me to join and become a Boy Scout out of the clear blue. I recall him owning a station wagon and him driving us on hiking trips and to Scout Camp that summer. He also invited the troop to his home to watch the basketball playoff game and the opening season of baseball the following April. The fact that sports were popular and that Mr. Meriwether lived around the corner from us with his family on Teasdale made visiting his home okay with my parents. When I told my dad about the visits, he put out his hand, smiled, and said, "Son, slap me five!"

Our already busy Scoutmaster became the coach for The Grace Gospel Midgets—our church's youth basketball team, which I joined along with my singing buddy Lawrence and Mr. Meriwether's son, Charles, Jr. Our coach had a cute daughter who gave us Zuzu chocolate cookies, Ginger snaps, and Ritz crackers with orange juice when watching TV at their house. She and the Ruff twin brothers are still associated with Grace Gospel Church to this day, along with Pat Lytle and Deacon Holmes, whose families all lived nearby.

In addition to basketball, music, and being Boy Scouts, Lawrence and I used our artistic creativity to draw and paint pictures. We also had hobbies, including building stick-model airplanes and kites that we flew on rooftops. Then, seeing other boys with scooters, we made our own using our Chicago roller skates attached to a two-by-four and an orange crate. We were proud of our creation and rode up and down the local streets with the other boys. Due to wanting Schwinn black panther bikes (that neither of our fathers could afford) to further our adventures of hanging out with the guys, we also built our own bicycles out of found used parts to ride to the Bronx Zoo and Pelham Bay Park. Desiring to have our own money, we carried A&P Supermarket food bags on weekends for senior adults, along with Daily Mirror newspaper routes on Sundays after church.

Along with those things, we were preparing to attend a school with a reputation for fighting outbreaks, so we had to be ready for the unknown with the mixture of Black, White, Italian, and Puerto Rican street gangs from all five NYC boroughs in attendance. While PS51 already had a fighting reputation among Black neighborhood street gangs, others were the Lightnings, Golden Guineas, the Counts, Gaylords, Diablos, and the Fordham Baldies. Gang fights were also had with the use of homemade zip guns. I learned to make them after the 3rd grade when I no longer wanted to wrestle with a smaller kid who could outdo all of us boys at the Forest House Community Center, where my sisters and I went after school. As it was with most 6th-grade boys heading to PS51 for the first time, I gathered with my close buddies to chat.

Interestingly, along with my singing friend Lawrence Wentz and Yaphet Kotto (who later became a famous Black actor), we also had an older buddy named Fred who was already attending PS51 and instructed us to always be with friends. Three other associates of ours were Philip Johnson (who knew both music and boxing), Dennis Birthright (a curly-haired kid who fought a lot), and Jimmy Harper (a boy from the south who could fight as well). After many discussions about life at PS51, we all felt comfortable.

As I continued to mature, I remained a relatively shy young man. Although I had already started to be more mindful of self-care, my buddy Jimmy Harper and I were talking about girls. One day, I met Jimmy's shy cousin Jean at his house. Jean was a cute pigeon-toed beauty I talked to about drawing. All the guys seemed to like her.

I recall swimming at Crotona Park with my buddies to check the girls out. I began feeling strongly attracted to a teenage beauty named Mary. She lived one block away from me on Boston Road. She was my first love experience. Although she adored me and allowed me to visit whenever her strict father was not home, she lovingly told me we could not have sex because I never had sex. While my feelings for her remained, at age 12, Jimmy talked me into having sex with an older girl by the same name. The boys called her "Fat Mary." On Saturdays, she let boys observe her showering from a nearby hallway window across the street from where I lived. That same group of boys told me to come and watch her, too. When Jimmy told her I was shy, she told him, "Tell him to come and visit me." I went to her—just as the other boys did—to prove I wasn't afraid. Afterward, I felt I had done something wrong, being a church kid and all.

Other things I learned to do to keep up with the boys just before turning 12 was hitching rides on the backs of trucks and trolly cars. It was fun...until my grandmother caught me and told my mom, who disciplined me. I also wore a cast on my arm due to falling from our park wall (I climbed it after the entrance was closed). I fractured it again after falling off the bike I had built. I also damaged my arm again after my 3rd-grade "Forest House" attitude changed. Not to be punked by a neighborhood bully named Harold Brown, who tried taking the bike I built, he ended up running home with a bloody nose when I hit him back. My mother made me apologize to him and his mother as well.

At the end of elementary school in June 1952, but before the summer break, two interesting things happened. On a very good note, I was presented with an Award of Merit for "Excellence in Art." That honor humbled me. Seeing that my artistic abilities were much like my mother's in her youth, my grandmother sent my 'Daily News' copy drawing of "Draw Me" back to them for a contest. What an exciting moment for me! Until...

A day of fun turned into a frightening, traumatic event for me. Just after getting my passing 6th-grade report card that June, I got arrested with Harold

Brown and three others for 'Juvenile Delinquency' after stealing Pepsi and Coke sodas from a Bronx delicatessen. We were chased by two detectives in plain clothes through that busy Bronx neighborhood. I hid underneath a parked car but was caught when the officer knelt and arrested me, putting me in handcuffs. Fear of going to jail and not graduating filled my very soul. We were taken to the precinct, where one of the detectives (who had coincidentally graduated from the same JHS we were headed to) spoke to us strictly about aiming toward our goals in order to succeed in life. We were then freed from police custody to our parents. Both of my parents were there at the time. They took me home, and my father disciplined me in his customary military form. Later, he promised to take me to Yankee Stadium for a special baseball game. Two days later, my mother took me down 3rd Avenue (under the 'L') to Alexanders and bought me a suit for my elementary school graduation. I remember it being the latest style, with a one-button Hollywood jacket and, of course, a complementary tie.

During that summer, just as my dad promised, he took me to see the Yankees play a double-header — also called the "Bronx Bombers." The players walked to the outfield bleachers between games, where I saw them in person. Four notables were Joe DiMaggio,

Billy Martin, shortstop Phil Rizzuto (whom I admired), and catcher Yogi Berra. All gave autographs to us kids. Much to my surprise, my dad bought me a Phil Rizzuto baseball glove from Devega Sporting Goods Store, where Billy Martin's father bought his. My father then took me to Macombs Dam Park across from Yankee Stadium on 161st Street and left me with older guys to observe and play baseball. Stunned by how my father did things but respecting the fact that he saw the potential in me to become a professional baseball player, I joined a local street baseball team known as "The Panthers" just to please him. Lawrence—my ace-boon coon—joined the team as well.

That September, when we entered 7th grade at the all-boys school, with our good grades and passed tests, Lawrence and I were put into music instrument classes. Lawrence went to the brass section to learn how to play the trombone. Oddly, I was placed in the string instrument class, learning how to play the violin. I was also allowed to take the instrument home to practice. Together, Lawrence and I played in the JHS band while, interestingly, music was exploding on WWRL Black Radio. Tommy Smalls was the first Black DJ in our area who had relocated to NYC from Georgia. His radio call name was "Dr. Jive." He hosted a weekday after-school radio show, where his opening slogan was, "Sit back and relax and enjoy the wax…from three-oh-five to five-three-oh…it's the Dr. Jive Show!"

At age 13, my dream to sing was on fire but not yet realized. Lawrence and I, as teenagers, were all the more motivated about vocal group singing, especially as we listened to the Dr. Jive show after school. I even observed my sister Gert and her girlfriends dancing with boys to the records played when our parents weren't home. When I asked where her friends came from, she told me about the nearby Bronx Elementary School (PS99) that she and her girlfriend Arlene went dancing at when our parents were home. She added that while the school had recreation for kids on Saturdays, the Dr. Jive Radio Show after school caused the flocking of kids of all ages to go there daily from 3 to 5 p.m. to have fun and dance.

Lawrence and I planned to hop on our bikes and go there as soon as the opportunity came. Once there, the two dances we observed while listening to Black vocal group records over the loudspeaker were 'The Grind' and 'The Walk.' They were the same dances my sister and her friends did with the boys at home. Simply put, 'The Grind' was a couple moving with each other closely without steps to a slow song. 'The

Walk' was also danced to slow songs, walking around the floor closely, like a smooth tango.

One of the beautiful love songs we all slow-danced to that whole year was a song called "You're Mine" by Dean Barlow and The Crickets, never knowing that I would meet their lead singer, Dean, years later. I learned they were also Bronx dudes who rehearsed in Morris High's schoolyard. What held my attention was the smooth bass singing that assisted Dean. When he sang the words "you're mine," the bass voice followed with "oh yes, you're mine." I continued to have a good listening ear for all the harmony parts and imitated the deep voice with Lawrence singing their soaring falsetto first tenor.

Coincidentally, another from the Bronx whom I came to know was Jimmy Keys of The Chords. He attended Morris High School and also rehearsed in PS 99. They came to be the key Black vocal group that crossed over to pop music radio stations with their first song, "Sh-Boom." Another was Lillian Leach, the sweet singing lead vocalist of The Mellows with the 1955 groovy ballads titled "Smoke from Your Cigarette" and "How Sentimental Can You Be." I also became acquainted with the smooth vocals of their cool bass singer, Mr. Arthur Crier. Yet another was Bobby Mansfield and The Wrens with the great love song "C'est La Vie." Not to leave out another pair of Bronx gentlemen, Robert & Johnny, who, as a duet, came out with "We Belong Together" — a song so powerfully loved that I even recorded it years later on my solo CD. Just around the corner from me on 164th Street lived Gene Redd of The Fi-Tones with two interesting songs titled "Foolish Dreams" and "Let's Fall in Love." I gravitated to listening to them through Gene's building's basement window. Regarding a 'small world,' Gene's piano player, Mr. Ruppert Brinker (who also played for The Chords and lived near my elementary school), I met in 1956 while on tour with my group when he played piano for The Platters with their huge hit song, "Only You."

Overall, for me, one of the many great vocal group songs that still grabs my attention due to its slow groove with a wavy first tenor that we all danced 'The Grind' to is "I" by The Velvets. Another is a 1952 love song hit that we danced both 'The Grind' and 'The Walk' that contained all the oncoming elements of Doo-Wop. The song is by The Vocaleers titled "Is It a Dream." I learned and sang it repeatedly and do so even to this day.

In 1954, Arthur Sterling, the manager of our Panthers baseball team, approached Lawrence and me on the sidewalk in front of my building as we worked on our bikes. Besides the fact that he lived around the corner from me, I did not know that he also played piano and knew about singing groups. He yelled, "Hey, James! Hey, Lawrence! I heard you two guys sing. Is that true?" Looking at each other, Lawrence and I stopped what we were doing, dropped our tools, stood straight up, and gave him our undivided attention. Arthur looked at us sternly and said, "James, do this: Ooh-bop-sha-doo." I did exactly what he asked in the same tone. He then asked Lawrence to do the same, which he did. Arthur then instructed us to sing our two parts simultaneously and, while doing so, added his voice. He then said, "Cut! That's three-part acapella harmony—or group singing without instruments!" While Lawrence and I were familiar with the term, something else he said confirmed both of our dreams. "Find skilled singers like yourselves and put a group together."

At the time, I did not realize those few words were going to spearhead a group music movement for kids, but I was excited nonetheless about that summer and moving forward with three other singers. Lawrence and I soon began identifying love song group harmony hits such as The Harptones singing "My Memories of You," The Strangers singing "My Friends," The Counts singing "Darling Dear," and The

Spaniels singing "Goodnight, Sweetheart, Goodnight."

Just before entering the 9th grade that September, my mother told my sisters and me that she was leaving our father. At age 14, I had already witnessed his negative, out-of-reach character with us—his family. In essence, we were already separated from him. Still, I was sadly disappointed. Also, my mother was pregnant when the announcement was made. After sharing the news with her mother, we moved in with her. Despite my familiarity with my grandmother's place and my aunt Edith, who also lived with her, it felt as if my dream was being delayed yet again. After all, my mom's well-being came first. And so, we left the Bronx.

CHAPTER 3: STITT JHS

During the first week of September 1954, before Labor Day, we relocated to our grandmother's three-bedroom apartment at 512 West 156th Street between Amsterdam and Broadway…without our father. As much as I thought I was, I was actually mentally unprepared for the transition. Living with five females as a growing teen, coupled with the constant reminder of specific painful experiences I had in that home, my only escape was taking Rex for walks.

While my memories were filled with being cared for by people other than my parents, one memory concerned my uncle Howard, who worked in a Harlem barbershop. When he visited one time, he was intoxicated. He waved his straight razor at me in a drunken rage, threatening to cut off my penis if I peed in his mother's bed again. Fortunately, I have a loving great-grandmother who bawled him out for his craziness.

Another memory concerned my cousin, Walter. He was assigned to watch my sisters and me when the adults weren't home. One day, while walking fast through the apartment with me on his shoulders, I fell to the floor because he refused to hold my hands. I ended up with a knot on my forehead — and a threat not to tell on him.

Of course, those guys knew my father was not in my life. I later found out that my mother's critical departure from him back to that very location on that September Labor Day weekend also served a purpose regarding my dream's destiny. It was, in fact, the very first day of school at my new JHS, Edward W. Stitt, PS164, that began to formally shape my future.

After walking up Amsterdam Avenue that first day with my mom and younger sister to Stitt's location on Edgecombe Avenue and 165th Street and completing my transfer information in their office, I made my way to room 313 — my 3rd-floor 9th-grade classroom. Once there, I was introduced to 25 nicely dressed girls and eight boys, all of whom were very familiar. The no-nonsense but pleasant teacher, Mrs. Smolar, informed the class that I was new to Stitt, having relocated to the area from the Bronx. In unison, they acknowledged me by saying, "Hi, James!"

We sat at combination desks separated by narrow aisles. I was seated to the right of Mrs. Smolar's desk in the next-to-last row by the windows. Just as the school bell rang, the classroom door swung open. Before the woolly-headed, 6'2", t-shirt-wearing, pigeon-toed, Tom Sawyer country boy-like youngster with high-water dungarees, no socks, and Pro-Ked sneakers dude could say a word, Mrs. Smolar calmly said, "Sherman Marlow Garnes, lateness is not tolerated. Not here."

He replied in a very deep voice, "Okay, teacher." That voice! I was blown away!

She then said, "As you know, Sherman, I'm Mrs. Smolar."

He responded in that same deep voice, "Yes, Mrs. Smolar. May I take my seat now?"

"You may," she answered. Although Sherman was a shy, laid-back, mild-mannered, giraffe-looking youngster, his deep bass voice got my attention immediately. Mrs. Smolar further instructed, "Sit in the last row by the windows next to James, a new boy in Stitt, and respectfully say good morning."

After doing so, the girls' voices were much friendlier than that of the boys as we all said, "Hi, Sherman!" Observing that exchange, I realized he was likable. No matter the teacher's reason, I was glad she seated him next to me, mainly for the opportunity to ask him about his deep voice.

As Mrs. Smolar prepared to teach, the idea came to me to ask Sherman about music. "His voice would be perfect for the bass harmony part of a new song by Hank Ballard and The Midnighters," I thought. So, as quietly as I could, I leaned toward him and whispered, "Can you sing bass?"

He responded with his mild-mannered deep voice, "Can you play basketball?"

Unmoved, I replied, "Yes. Have you heard the vocal group son "Annie Had a Baby… She Can't Work No More"?"

Our brief exchange ended when Sherman said, "Show me."

After asking him to call me Jimmy, not James, our friendship was born. I was assured that my dream COULD be realized by knowing he, too, had a musical ear, enabling me to show him bass-tenor harmony.

That important day was when I met Sherman, the first of three other ninth graders who became the actual beginning of our superstar vocal group. Before that reality, however, when the four of us became a popular quartet in the neighborhood through and beyond 9th grade, a student was entering the 8th grade who became our lead singer in that Washington Heights school building (which is still there).

Moving along...

As I came to know Sherman better, I felt almost immediately that our friendship was the start of TWO DREAMERS coming together with one common goal: stardom. My dream was further aided at the dawn of the vocal group craze when two songs exploded onto the scene that year: "Sh-Boom" by The Chords and "Earth Angel" by The Penguins.

Sherman was a light-skinned boy with keen features and freckles — unheard of on a Black person. He could have passed for White were it not for his woolly hair. He had an afro before afros even came out! However, it was his low-key personality, deep southern drawl, and height that made him who he was. When he stepped into the classroom that first day, it looked like he had just quietly gotten up that morning, jumped into his outgrown clothes, slipped his feet into his size 13 ½ high-top sneakers, grabbed his notebook, and moseyed out of his house headed to school. LATE. The school was just across the street from his building. From the classroom windows on our side, he could see into his living room and kitchen windows. But, as it was with most kids, like my Bronx buddy Lawrence, while Sherman was a smart student, his focus was on his dream: basketball. Specifically, he dreamt of becoming a Harlem Globetrotters player (I later learned his father had taken him to try out for the team).

Being too young for pro basketball, yet knowing the game with the unequaled ability for his age, Sherman signed up with the Stitt JHS team that October. He also played with older boys in the neighborhood on a Harlem team called Toots Rivets. Directly across the street from his apartment building's entrance and Stitt JHS, there was a small outdoor basketball court that was part of Edgecombe Avenue Park. There, I watched him with older guys dribble and dunk a basketball like Globetrotter players Marcus Haines and Meadowlark Lemon.

On weekends, Sherman and I goofed around and frolicked while he palmed his basketball. It was then that his inner antics and the fun side of him became apparent. He was a tall, good-looking kid who wowed people whenever and wherever he played, but he was also a natural comedian who could coolly imitate folks. He had me cracking up, no matter where we were.

The basketball court in Edgecombe Park extends from a group of benches just across from Stitt. It was there that I loaded Sherman up at lunchtime with singing information. Along with basketball and being popular, he humbly knocked the socks off girls, all while becoming my ace-boon-coon buddy, discussing our desires and dreams. It seemed we were engaged in a "dreamer's battle" of sorts. He was fascinated with basketball, and a vocal harmony group was my dream—something in me that he saw clearly. I shared with him that vocal groups had been ongoing since the late '40s and that the Black vocal group fad happening in New York, Philadelphia, Chicago, and Los Angeles was bringing forth something called "Doo-Wop."

As time progressed, I explained that in order to make specific singing points without unaffordable instruments, 'neighborhood cronies' like he and I could use goofy-like nonsense syllable wordings in place of rhythmic punctuation, which, in fact, changed the music game. I told him it basically started as a type of home-grown quartet singing thing, mainly in a family known as the incomparable Mills Brothers, who became highly influential with their most known early hit, "Till Then." The group was also advanced musically, singing barbershop and gospel. While "Till Then" was slow and sad, it had a smooth, groovy rhythm accentuated by piano, guitar, and drums. The

Mills Brothers were also the first to compose songs mimicking harmonicas, cymbals, horns, bass, and drum instruments. They even used nonsense wording with their voices, which I demonstrated for Sherman. I informed him that this stuff was moving fast in neighborhoods and schools and that, for me, it started in the Bronx, listening to my father's records — copying and jamming acapella with radio groups and a buddy of mine and three others just before my transfer to Stitt.

Since I had Sherman's continued attention, I went on to share that while a White vocal group, The Four Freshmen, sang songs like "The Day Isn't Long Enough," they alerted and sharpened my ability to hear harmony at age 12. Furthermore, the most recent Black vocal group attention-getter, The Harptones, produced a smooth love song titled "My Memories of You." When I showed him harmony using a tenor and then the bass part to both songs, he was stunned and wanted to know more. "Show me how," he said.

That next day, I took him to hear the very song I referenced the day we first met in our 9th-grade classroom: "Annie Had a Baby...She Can't Work No More" — the 1954 #1 R&B hit by Hank Ballard and The Midnighters. There was a small shop on Amsterdam loaded with kids that was located around the corner from our school, where I took him at lunchtime. As it was with all soda fountain and ice cream parlors during that time that sold candy and cold-cut sandwiches, it also had a jukebox. I explained to Sherman that the young crowd was there due to attention-getting songs that first flowed from radios, attracting kids of all ages. While most adults paid little attention as they enjoyed the Rock 'n' Roll explosion, the youth gravitated toward the vocal group craze.

As he watched, I inserted a nickel into the slot of the jukebox, pushed a rectangular button, and a 78 record inside lifted from its rack and was gently placed onto the turntable. As that R&B record blasted out of the jukebox's speaker and others on the wall, kids rollicked and danced while eating their sandwiches. Sherman watched the activity around him, totally moved by it all. Then, after showing him the sexy, catchy bassline first-tenor duet I came up with to follow the lead singer's words, he got it! I continued to come up with other two-part harmony ideas, like the one with a very cool set of words from another new hit record called "The Marriage" by The Solitaires, "Yes, I'll say that I do…if you say I do, too." Before October came, Sherman and I sang our tenor-bass duet combination, listening for acoustic echoes in building hallways, lobbies, elevators, subways, and, of course, walking through trains to get attention from girls.

Then, the first weekend of October, while walking from Sherman's house to Bill's Grocery Store on the corner of 165th and Amsterdam for his mother, that little 12-year-old pre-teen, Frankie, that I referenced earlier (who knew Sherman) threw his high tenor in with mine (he, of course, came into the picture later). Looking way up at Sherman, Frankie said, "I've been watching you two cats harmonize up and down the street, and, as you know, while I can also sing, I'm gonna be famous!"

Sherman, being one of few words, looked down at Frankie and simply said, "We'll see."

Frankie, while cute and smart, was also snooty. He moved close to Sherman, looked up at him (with his right hand above his eyes), and said, "What you gonna be when you grow up? Huh, man?"

Looking down at Frankie, Sherman spoke one word: "Later." He then turned and walked away. As we headed down the street, he said to me, "That kid also sang with two others. One of them was his brother."

The vocal group excitement among teens was insatiable. There were two other boys in our class who instantly joined up with Sherman and me to sing in the boys' room at Stitt: Dennis Birthright (who, with his vicious vocals, could make his baritone voice sound like a horn), and Charles Wheeler (whose second-tenor voice came off like a flute). Singing freelance harmonizing vocals had us so mentally magnetized in the park that we mistakenly took it into the classroom one day. Mrs. Smoler had to put her foot down but also realized that vocal group singing had become a bug, even in schools. Standing before her were four boys loaded with musical potential, so she excused our "mishap" as we showed her respect. In fact, when the movie "Blackboard Jungle" was released, with its Black schoolteacher and White students, music exploded with a milestone release hit song by Bill Haley and The Comets titled "Rock Around the Clock."

By then, the landmark hit song "Earth Angel" by The Penguins was already out and had become the #1 R&B/Rock 'n' Roll hit song in America. Its pop-like sound caused the music to cross over to pop charts, strengthening Doo-Wop worldwide. The Black vocal group movement was further bolstered by gaining love song attention from females and hooking teenage boys to sing. My personal attraction to that song was that while it had more of an upbeat for a slow song, the lyrics of the lead voice lent to his innocence when he sang, "I'm just a fool…a fool in love…with you." In addition, accompanying his sincere, clean-cut, laid-back singing style with humility and a heavenly song title, his love for his "Earth Angel" was made very clear. Also, the group's nicely placed unison and background harmony behind the lead singer's main question, "My darling dear, will you be mine?" rounded out the song's message.

Another 9th-grader whom Sherman and I grouped with while in Edgecombe Park at lunchtime was Howard "Howie" Jenkins. No one could tell him he wasn't the coolest boy on the planet. He truly had a terrific lead voice and knew exactly how to use it to draw girls over to us as we sang "Earth Angel" with him. That was a cool know-how (musically speaking). He was someone I knew mainly by face because his team played against ours during the basketball tournament that October. There was one problem: Sherman said Howie wasn't a team player. Like Sherman, I observed Howie's very showy personality during lunch, which also found its way onto the basketball court.

However, Howie was always anxious to form a vocal group. He brought together four others, including myself (falsetto first-tenor), Sherman (bass), Dennis (baritone), and Julius Philips (second tenor, who also sang lead). The first song we sang continually was "The Glory of Love" by The Five Keys—a song I learned in the Bronx. Five others were "Crying in the Chapel" (The Orioles), "Story Untold" (The Nutmegs), "Gloria" (The Cadillacs), "A Sunday Kind of Love" and "Life is But a Dream" (The Harptones). Still, "Earth Angel" was our most recognizable 'hit,' due to its strong attraction.

As a 'group,' we were excited about the potential to get discovered, which, at that time, was the primary aim of newly-formed vocal groups like The Moonglows—a Louisville, Kentucky group that, through an impressed singer friend, came to know Alan Freed (a White Cleveland, Ohio DJ who got started in 1951 with WJW Radio). Then, beginning in September 1954, he became well-known with his so-called "Moon Dog Show" in NYC on WINS Radio, which led to him doing Brooklyn and NY Paramount shows. While he first played heavy blues primarily, his show was also the first of its kind to bring Black music to White teenagers. To fit his "Moon Dog Show," he gave The Moonglows their name. Although he first recorded them, they didn't gain true recognition until they switched to Chess Records in Chicago, recording a string of hits starting with

"Sincerely" that November. The guys I got together with basically lasted through early December, mainly practicing "Earth Angel" in the boys' room at lunchtime, tightening our harmony.

When the weather permitted, we'd sing in Edgecombe Park, just across from Stitt's two front doors. While doing so, we attracted neighboring folks — both young and old — along with Stitt students. Once, as we were deeply involved with singing and attracting girls, we didn't hear the school lunch bell ring, telling us it was time to return to class. That day, Mrs. Smolar was on 'lunch duty.' She blew her whistle from the front steps of Stitt, but we didn't hear her. Realizing her whistle failed to get our attention, she hollered, "HEY! YOU EARTH ANGELS! GET IN HERE! NOW!" As the girls rushed in, slapping 'five' with each other, we did the same. With that excitement, along with the teacher calling us five boys "You Earth Angels," we began referring to ourselves as The Earth Angels. Disappointingly, after December, our Stitt group was no more.

One of the boys had to relocate with his family, and Sherman stated, "Howie's always being too showy, wanting all the attention. Plus, he doesn't see eye-to-eye with us like a team player," so we dissipated. In fact, Sherman, being very bothered by

Howie, quit the group first, just as the excitement grew about me breaking him into singing the great bass lead on a song that was released that November by The Drifters titled "White Christmas."

Sherman was a bold team player on the basketball court, but I saw his humility when I took him to meet my family. When he invited me to his house to meet his family, I remember his mother cooking southern soul food that blew me away!

Even though The Earth Angels were no more, when Sherman and I got into another group, Howie wanted to join us on the stage at our Stitt JHS June 1955 pre-graduation prom event. Because he showed humility when I shared how I felt about him being a "one-man show" type of performer, I told him I would try to make it happen. I quickly realized that The Earth Angels weren't meant to be. My sights were still set on my own dream of getting ON STAGE with a group. Nonetheless, performing at that great Audubon Ballroom location was at least fruitful and enlightening.

Through it all, there is something of importance to note here. A musician named Richard White entered the picture. He was a friendly, big-brother type of gentleman toward Sherman, who happened to live on the first floor of his building. At times, he played basketball with us and uplifted us both concerning our dreams. After learning about our failed The Earth Angels group, he said, "Never give up on your dreams. They come for a purpose." Sherman and I looked at each other, not quite understanding Richard's second point. That's when he stated, "When you two guys get another group, I'll help you with original songs." We didn't take his offer seriously at first, but his encouragement about forming another group had already begun happening heading into that Christmas holiday and into 1955.

At the time, Sherman was already establishing himself with a Puerto Rican 9th grader named Joe Negroni. Joe was forming a group with his buddy and wanted Sherman to sing bass with them. His buddy, Herman Santiago (also a 9th grader), coincidently lived just around the corner from Sherman on 165th Street. Both observed Sherman and me doing our duets and singing with The Earth Angels in Edgecombe Park. Sherman wanted me to think about joining up with them, too. Although they were friendly and cool Puerto Ricans (I wasn't prejudiced in the least), I wondered how Sherman could be interested in singing with two Latin guys, especially where Doo-Wop was concerned.

Sherman explained, "The main one, Joe Negroni, is into both music and, most importantly, show business. His buddy, Herman Santiago, has a good lead voice. Joe's name for his dream group is...The Ermines."

CHAPTER 4: THE ERMINES

In February 1955, I turned 15 and was still without any idea whatsoever of how my dream would become a reality. Sherman and I remained close friends, joking and laughing about others as youngsters often do. Even as our sights were set on our June graduation and possibly attending college thereafter, all around, singing groups were bursting onto the scene and performing at theatres like the Apollo, the Lowe's, and Brooklyn's the Fox and the Paramount. The mere possibility that my group singing dreams would one day SOON come to pass was laser-beam focused on an unknown future.

As my dream's flames grew, my mother birthed my beautiful third sister, Alice, leading our piano-playing Uncle Francis to promise her his nearby apartment on Edgecombe Avenue and 155th Street. Notably, other well-known Black celebrities lived there as well. My uncle had departed for Los Angeles in search of better work and then sent for his wife and daughter after purchasing a home that Nat King Cole formerly owned. Mr. Cole gave my uncle his piano, and my uncle gave me his. Imagine my amazement that following November, when we moved into my uncle's old apartment, and there stood a Baby Grand piano that I could call my own!

I recall Mrs. Smolar asking me to use my artistic ability for a specific project at school. My drawing skills were used on our entire schoolroom's back blackboard to colorfully display all nine planets, from the sun to Pluto. Sherman helped with that project. When the basketball season ended in mid-March, Sherman remained drawn to singing with the other two 9th-graders, Joe Negroni and Herman Santiago — The Ermines — and continued asking me to consider joining the trio.

I found a couple of things "odd" about Sherman's insistence that I lend my voice to the group: 1. The group's name (I had nothing against Joe, as he knew show business and also wanted me in his group), and 2. Joe and his buddy were Puerto Ricans. Up to that point, I had not heard of ANY Latinos singing vocal group R&B or Blow Harmony (slow love songs), as we Black guys called it on the street. My passion for music was completely realized by the sounds of Doo-Wop, the chord changes, and those passionate words of love behind each song's message. I refused to allow anyone or anything to come between my dream and me.

In his attempts to further convince me, Sherman shared that while Joe knew about Rock 'n' Roll, R&B, and vocal groups, he also knew all about Black groups, particularly as they moved into Pop music. Fully convinced about Sherman's desire to have me join The Ermines, I agreed — but not without feeling out Joe and his intentions as soon as we formally met. Due to his living conveniently three blocks from me on 153rd Street between the same two avenues (Amsterdam and Broadway), we began serious talks as we walked back and forth to school. He used that time to give me a deeper knowledge of how show business worked.

Joe was an Italian-looking Puerto Rican with a pretty-boy, rockabilly hairstyle (like the American actor Tony Curtis) with a cool appearance. At times, he wore colorful t-shirts under his jacket, saddle-stitch peg pants, and Flag-Flyer shoes with pop-up clips to open them. Along with being a follower of James Dean of the great movies "East of Eden" and "Rebel Without a Cause" (with Natalie Wood and Sal Mineo (a hot star at the time)), he also knew a lot about Horror films. For example, he shared with me that Lon Chaney, Sr. was innovative in make-up artistry and did his own in the movie "The Hunchback of Notre Dame." Soon enough, I learned Joe was far from being a show business dummy. He was also mature for his age —

only five months older than I—and gave himself a "Hollywood name": Lance Sterling. Wow!

Joe—being a sure-of-himself playboy who could get virtually any girl he wanted—totally blew my mind one day when he shared a story about an attractive, untouchable, light-skinned Black Catholic girl down the block from Stitt that ALL of us boys craved. The mind-blowing fact was that she met up with him secretly!

What mainly caught my attention about Joe, besides his maturity, was his sincerity concerning visions, desires, and dreams. He knew exactly how to accomplish all of them. Along with his overall eye-opening, across-the-board superior show business knowledge, he declared that the White Rock 'n' Roll phenomenon had opened the doors for anyone with consistent fame aspirations. Wanting to impress me musically, Joe showed off his DJing skills by imitating DJ Alan Freed while playing "Rock Around the Clock" by Bill Haley and The Comets—and impressed me, he did!

Amid the flurry of information gathered from Joe, vocal group singing remained the key to my future. He talked to me about vocal groups such as the Ames Brothers and Four Aces, who had a huge hit called "Love Is a Many Splendid Thing." He also mentioned Billy Vaughn and The Hilltoppers, The Three Chuckles (with singer-songwriter Teddy Randazzo), and The Crew Cuts.

With as much seriousness as I could muster, I responded, "They're all White! The Crew Cuts redid "Life Could Be a Dream," which was better known as "Sh-Boom" by a Black group from my Bronx neighborhood called The Chords. Although the White group's version held the #1 spot on Pop charts, their version stinks."

Not to be outdone, Joe replied, "While some of the White groups did better than Black ones, overall, they aided the vocal group movement when they copied and covered key Black vocal group hit songs that had drawing power. Of course, it didn't hurt when, as a result of both Black and White females loving both the words and group lead singers, those songs became big hits! Just think about the reactions of the female listeners when Willie Winfield sang "Sunday Kind of Love" with his group, The Harptones."

Joe was correct. There was no denying the power of "change" in the music industry!

Wanting Sherman to recognize that Joe truly had excellent vocal group knowledge, even while lacking that certain 'Black mood-harmony feel' like The Mellows, Orioles, Velvets, and Vocaleers, I needed to find a way to highlight Joe's actual potential. After all, if that likable Latino could come to feel genuine Black vocal group harmonies such as what I was drawn to in the Bronx via radio, street groups, and Harlem jukeboxes, it seemed getting down to vocal group business with him was not far out of reach...and could get me even closer to my dream. If Joe could truly sing heartfelt vocal group harmony like that of The Earth Angels and was serious about getting attention and being discovered, I was willing and ready to give him a try.

What I liked most about Joe was his fame insight. I recall him saying, "The key thing born in the hearts of most soul brother groups that led to hit records was them sticking to their desires and dreams." That very statement sealed the deal. Right away, we became friends—a component of our relationship that never changed.

Sherman—being very uplifted about me feeling good regarding Joe's musical expertise—then shared details about Joe's singing friend, Herman, whom he had known longer due to him living down the street from Sherman across from Stitt. "Herman is a well-liked Puerto Rican. While he's already Joe's lead singer, they're auditioning background singers at his house during lunch and after school. You might consider helping them," he advised. Sherman added that Joe and Herman had observed me showing guys group harmony at lunchtime from the front steps of Stitt. When he said that, I recalled seeing them as I sang with The Earth Angels. At one point, Joe casually mentioned it but did not harp on needing a guy with superb harmony skills like me.

Although Sherman and I goofed about a Negro-Puerto Rican harmony mix and the weird group name, The Ermines, that Joe wanted for his group, Sherman reminded me about Richard White's words: "Don't give up on your dreams." In fact, Richard saw us singing together and coming and going so often, he further encouraged us when he added that he had poems and short love notes written by a female friend that he wanted to give us to compose original songs. Initially, Sherman and I found his suggestion funny and off-beat, not realizing at the time the enormous, monumental value that one of those notes would turn out to be for us. *Why Do Fools Fall in Love* was a song born from a love note that became our historic musical masterpiece.

Getting back to The Ermines...

Sherman commented, "C'mon, Jimmy. Don't mind the group's name. Joe is a dreamer, just like you." So, after seeing what Joe was all about, I decided to learn more about their singing buddy, Herman Santiago.

At the end of March, I accepted Joe and Sherman's offer. The four of us joined forces—Joe, Sherman, Herman, and I—and met at Herman's house during a school lunch break, where I promised to aid them with auditioning singers.

Herman—a B+ student one year older than me—was already shaving with a mannish quality about himself but was quieter than Joe. He loved music, but baseball and basketball were most often topics of our discussions. He, in fact, bought his first-base baseball glove with money earned by carrying supermarket packages for people. I shared with him that I did the same job in the Bronx, but my dad had purchased my Phil Rizzuto glove. "I already tried out to be a professional ballplayer at Yankee Stadium, but I am too short for first base. I play shortstop and outfield," Herman stated.

"Wow!" I thought.

The first time I ate Spanish food was at Herman's house during that lunchtime meeting. Thinking I had not eaten, he offered me some of his mother's cooking. Sherman, being a hefty eater, was already in the refrigerator. To Herman, he said, "Hurry and warm up some of your mom's leftover rice and beans for Jimmy." Joe and I said nothing as Herman politely motioned for us to sit at the kitchen table.

Along with Herman being polite, he also attracted older women. There was one who lived in the corner building of his block. He first started carrying packages for her and then was later enticed to "stay a little longer" after bringing them up to her 4th-floor apartment. Sherman and I later teased him about her continuously wanting his undivided attention. Still, like Joe, he tried staying private about those things, even after delaying our rehearsal once by not coming right back down. He did, however, have a clean way about himself. He was always prepared and groomed for school, wearing a suit and tie that he bought with his own money. Also, feeling inhibited due to his Spanish accent, he rarely spoke Spanish around us and kept a bilingual dictionary on hand in his back pocket. As boys do, Sherman, Joe, and I goofed about that, too.

Two days later, three singers auditioned at Herman's house at 3:15, right after school. Their efforts were to no avail. Two of them—Pitman and Hector—could not sing harmony or even hear a precise musical tone that I pitched in their ears as they tried singing with Herman, Joe, and Sherman. The third guy, Hurley, could hear harmony but wanted to do his own thing when he was tasked with singing a fixed harmony line. By 4:00, those auditions were over, and the three boys left Herman's house.

Today, as I reflect on that day, I see that as Joe, Sherman, and Herman observed me teaching, they quietly observed my ability to assign various musical tones to singers based on their voice range as either a soprano, alto, tenor, baritone, or bass. Additionally, while doing so, I now see that I was the one auditioning...for them.

By the end of March, our four-boy Negro-Puerto Rican group, The Ermines, was officially off and running.

Concerning our odd group name, The Ermines: Joe and I understood that while Doo-Wop was primarily a homegrown urban music title given to slow love songs and up-tempo jumps and was closely related to Rock 'n' Roll dance music hit song groups of Black origin, it covered a vast area of vocal group titles. Some that come to mind are:

- Soldiers – "The Cadets"
- Flowers – "The Carnations"
- Cars – "The Cadillacs"
- Cosmetics – "The Avons"
- Card-playing – "The Jacks" and "The Solitaires"
- Birds – "The Ravens," who set the stage for The Flamingos, Orioles, Swallows, Robins, Cardinals, Meadowlarks, Pelicans, Larks, Crows, and Penguins. (The Penguins' great hit song, "Earth Angel," became my first vocal group's title, The Earth Angels.)

Although we were referred to as "Street Corner Singers," Joe favored his odd, Eurasian, short-tailed weasel title, The Ermines.

Throughout the month of April, while Black groups had become prominent with music driven by boys who followed and copied them, I, too, was continually humming harmony in the ears of our guys, loading them up with specific ways to copy songs. Due to radio stations WINS, WLIB, WNJR, and WWRL playing Doo-Wop hits constantly, we gravitated toward acapella singing on the Edgecombe Park bench just across from Sherman's building. It never ceased to amaze me how Stitt boys and girls were drawn to watch us "perform" during lunch and after school.

While we loved the attention, especially from the girls attracted to our looks as two light-skinned Blacks and two cool Spanish boys singing Doo-Wop love songs, I reflected on the time spent watching my dad at age five to becoming a popular local vocal group at age 15 with The Ermines. Our popularity was confirmed one day by Mr. Earth Angel himself, Howard Jenkins, whom I saw quietly observing us. He was low-key about wanting to sing lead with us at our first upcoming Audubon Ballroom Stitt Graduate dance show in June. One day, he respectfully told me, "Don't let nothing stop you, Jimmy. You're an important part of The Ermines." Those words felt good to hear. I responded by telling him the girls would love to see him with us as well.

Despite certain singing fears that Herman had with his slight Puerto Rican accent, I felt he had a convincing style when singing lead on our first learned song, "Why Don't You Write Me" by The Jacks. He presented it like it was his own. Another cool thing was, knowing about Jazz, like me, aided his singing style and phrasing.

I constantly worked to perfect our group's harmony with countless songs while singing first tenor, along with other parts where needed. Joe most often sang baritone in our group. He loved to do the very showy Buddy Holly and Gene Vincent songs, but they weren't ideal for us. Sherman's bass singing was a humdinger.

We did a pretty song with Herman as the lead: "Heaven in Paradise" by Don Julian & The Meadowlarks (with Sherman's incredible bridge bass line). Another was "That's What's You're Doing to Me" by Clyde McPhatter and The Dominoes, with Sherman, Joe, and me in the background, saying, "Hey, pretty baby…can't you see…that's what you're doing to me?" Yet another memorable song was "You Painted Pictures" by The Spaniels, on which Joe sang an excellent lead. Singing songs acapella was very fulfilling for us, especially as we sang other '50s hits like "Have Mercy, Baby" by Billy Ward and The Dominoes, "Hey, Senorita" by The Penguins, and "Lily Mabelle" by The Valentines. In fact, Richard Barrett (that group's lead singer) was the one who discovered our group to record. He also played a distinguished role in our lives after doing so.

The following month (May), for echo/acoustic sound purposes, we sang in Sherman's building hallway. Even then, we were primarily referred to as 'street corner singers' who often performed on the corner of 165th and Amsterdam, where Bill's Excel-o-Mart Grocery Store was located.

Speaking of 'street corner groups,' five guys known as The Capitols popped into our lives at that time. In fact, one named MacDonald lived in the apartment building next to Stitt, directly across the street from Herman, where Sherman and I saw them exiting and singing as we walked down the block. While Sherman and Herman knew those older guys (who became our singing group's aides), they were already singing a super-polished R&B song acapella, which completely mesmerized me — and I later used. The day Sherman introduced me to them, I was pleasantly surprised to know they were already familiar with who I was. I met MacDonald (bass), Alvin (lead), Harry (baritone), and Bobby Tesman (first tenor), who later introduced us to his girlfriend, Lorraine Clark, who had fallen in love with our group and who further aided my dream.

After observing us singing on the street corner, Lorraine was drawn to us and instantly became interested in managing us. Surprisingly, she was friends with one of The Penguins of "Earth Angel" fame. She told Bobby that when The Penguins came to

NYC to perform at the Apollo Theatre that September, she wanted us to meet the gentleman she knew. Joe and I were floored!

Back to The Capitols...

When I asked them about not being seen singing on the street in our area, Bobby (a barbershop guy) said they sang further down on Harlem's streets. They were very popular there and looking to record their original songs. I learned that they rehearsed at Stitt's after-school Night Center—a place Herman had suggested we think about using as well, due to his mom needing us to find somewhere else to rehearse. Herman also attended the Night Center regularly during the week, playing ping-pong with the female manager of a summer baseball team. The rest of us decided to join, both for the love of baseball and his sake. Since Herman knew The Capitols, he wanted me to get to know them and gain more musical insight. When I did, their bass singer, MacDonald (well-versed in music scenarios), shared with me that rehearsing at Stitt's Night Center was beneficial for them. The group could work without interference and get things done quickly and privately. Most importantly, he explained that I needed to quickly get into working on original songs for The Ermines—something that was desperately needed on our way to being discovered.

A gentleman named Elder oversaw the Stitt Night Center. I met him through my older sister Gert, who liked him. Joe spoke to him regarding setting up a room for us in the evenings to rehearse. After their discussion, we were given a rehearsal room in Stitt's basement school machine shop. I spoke with Joe about our group's rapid growth, and we began to move forward with professional eyes overlooking our every move, particularly regarding moving toward the stage and composing original songs to record. As we got rolling during our Stitt evening hours three times a week, I remained focused on my schoolwork and helping my mother and grandmother at home, all while beginning to make up and write possible original songs that I noted in my Ermines rehearsal notebook.

Along with my ear for music already in place, showing our group the basic 1-6-2-5 chord progression used in mostly all '50s Doo-Wop and R&B music slow hit songs, importantly, I also watched The Capitols. In doing so, I realized that they, too, wrote original songs like the radio singing groups we copied.

I was well on my way to composing an original slow song idea with simple, soothing harmonies and words of love (that always got the listeners' attention).

A very beautiful slow song was birthed from my efforts that I named "Please Be Mine." Like other songwriters, its title was inspired by the words of "Earth Angel":

"Earth Angel...Earth Angel...will you be mine? My darling dear...love you all the time." The lead singer's following words, "I'm just a fool...a fool in love with you," influenced the title of our hit song, *Why Do Fools Fall in Love*. That song was the key side of our first 78 record, with *Please Be Mine* on its flip side. After showing Herman the simple "Please Be Mine" words of love to sing the lead, he got right into it.

Another song we later recorded (written by Joe) was also influenced by "Earth Angel." The title was "Am I Fooling Myself Again." Then, interestingly, I got a strong idea from a song that The Capitols sang titled "Come On, Baby." The cool thing about that song was that it had the line, "I love you, baby, and I want you to be my girl," which led me to name my concept of a medium-fast song idea, "I Want You to Be My Girl." That song had tight Doo-Wop harmony and became our second biggest hit.

Stitt's Night Center was where we worked in private on original songs, but Sherman's hallway lobby was where we came up with 'stage steps,' all while we also concentrated on our echoes within the semi-wide area just a few steps beyond the front doors. When we sang even louder, the ornamental chandeliers surrounding the inner lights would seemingly shimmer even brighter, energizing our stage performance thoughts and, of course, my dream of possible fame as The Ermines...even as residents both coming and going called us "Hallway Boys."

CHAPTER 5: WHY DO FOOLS FALL IN LOVE

As Rock 'n' Roll and vocal group music increased near the end of May 1955, our group continued to evolve and improve. As we looked toward graduation from Stitt JHS to George Washington High School, the remarkable song that led to our group's instant greatness, *Why Do Fools Fall in Love*, came to us in the form of a love note.

One Saturday afternoon, around 2:00 after baseball practice, while Sherman and I waited for Joe and Herman on the Edgecombe Park bench, we talked about our after-graduation dance event. When the rain started falling seemingly out of nowhere, we ran across the street into Sherman's building, where our pre-fame musical moment came to be. It was a moment that led our group to also being the beginners of the phenomenal youth movement in music, along with world-renowned fame—and it all began with Sherman's big brother friend, Mr. Richard White, handing us his lady friend's love notes out of which came the song *Why Do Fools Fall in Love*.

Richard White had become a constant in our lives after observing us singing harmony in his building as members of The Earth Angels and The

Ermines, and he was even one of those people who referred to us as "Hallway Boys." Being a working musician himself, he wanted to do something special for us. As he entered the building that Saturday, he asked Sherman, "Where are they?"

"Nearby," came Sherman's reply in his distinguished deep voice. Sherman and I glanced at each other, each of us likely thinking the same thing: Richard White was prepared to hand over his promised one-page love notes for our group! Our eyes followed Richard to his apartment—#1A—which was just into the lobby to our left. After he fully entered, we both turned toward the front doors and saw Herman and Joe rush in out of the rain. Sherman and I quickly shared with them what was about to occur concerning Richard's promise before going inside his apartment.

Richard returned, demanding our immediate attention. "Due to the current hot vocal group movement and the progress you guys have made putting together original songs to make records, I now desire to aid you four boys by giving you these special poetic love notes that rhyme." Regarding the writer of them, whom Richard never found necessary to mention, we saw for ourselves a name inscribed under each: Delores Green. There were about a dozen romantic, poetic one-page love notes. Some were typed, and others were handwritten. Some were on lined paper, others on unlined notepad paper. Still, it was apparent that something else was on Richard's mind at that moment: the desire to see the four of us boys succeed — and those love notes were gifts to us four singing boys that came from the mysterious Delores Green's heart to Richard's heart...to ours.

Before proceeding with telling how the construction of the love note that became *Why Do Fools Fall in Love* came to be, I feel more about Ms. Delores Green must be made known. In fact, there were truths I learned over 60 years later during a telephone conversation with Sherman's sister, Mearl.

Along with Delores being the writer of those love notes, Mearl told me about a few other handwritten one-pagers that only she saw. When I asked her for more information and how she knew about them, she said, "While Delores Green was a very nice young lady, she was **MRS.** Delores Green. She had a child that I babysat in 1954." Interestingly, what tied everything together concerning Richard White living in the building was that **MRS.** Delores Green lived on the 4th floor *of the same building!*

Mearl concluded by sharing that Delores wanted her poetic writings published but never told her about giving them to Richard White. Mearl learned from Sherman how *Why Do Fools Fall in Love* came to be after it became our first big hit song (in January 1956), and one of Delores' love notes was its inspiration. (More specifically, that love note was turned into a slow song **written by me** six months earlier.) While Sherman might have known that Richard received Mrs. Green's love notes to help her in some way, he was also aware that Richard helped others, just as he did with our group at that time. Lastly, Mearl stated that she knew Richard was a very busy, unmarried gentleman with no time for girlfriends. *Seemingly.*

Getting back to the story...

After receiving the love notes from Richard White, the four of us boys couldn't wait to begin writing and singing our own original songs. At first, we stood in the hallway, joking and laughing about the mushy content of the notes. Admittedly, we knew nothing about love or what was to come. Our commotion outside his door prompted Richard to come back to us with a serious look on his face. We immediately hushed and looked at him as he said, "I foresee you boys making a great record and establishing yourselves as a known singing group. Along with the songs you've already made up, these true, original love notes — or poems of love — that I've given you will aid your quest even moreso. That's my hope. So, stay with working on originals. Time is of the essence. Okay?" Before returning to his apartment, he turned once more to look directly at Sherman and said, "I told you before about sticking with your dream." Then, looking at all four of us, he added, "Guys, never give up on your dreams. They have a purpose."

At the time, those poetic notes seemed of little importance, especially in light of us already working on our originals. Herman (feeling that The Ermines were 'the property' of Joe and him) thought that he should be the one to hold onto them. However, Joe (knowing Herman's lack of musical ability compared to mine) said, "No, Herman. As you already know, Jimmy's musical ability and creativity got us moving and into doing original songs." Joe, also knowing the business aspect of songwriting, said, "Most critically, we need to make sure we get our own songs copywritten to be legally covered financially. If any of our original songs were ever recorded by us for a record company, whomever the writers are will also begin receiving songwriter royalties. That is, of course, aside from singer's royalties."

The following fact must be mentioned here and will be reemphasized later in its fullest context: The night we were asked by George Goldner, "Who wrote *Why Do Fools Fall in Love?*" after its final recording, I spoke up and replied, "We all did." Then, when Mr. Goldner stated we would all get credit but that only two last names out of the five of us could be put on the record itself, Herman stated, "Lymon and Santiago." When the record was released a month later (the first week of January 1956, as a 78 record), its label read 'Lymon-Santiago-Goldner.' Although it was common for producers (i.e., Mr. Goldner) to add their names to songs created and written by others in those days, it was a grave mistake made by Herman not to give him two of the four names that the original words of *Why Do Fools Fall in Love* should have been credited to.

Getting back to the moment in Sherman's lobby hallway, deciding on who should hold onto Delores Green's love notes...

After rejecting Herman's suggestion, Joe asked me if I would be interested in holding onto her writings for safekeeping — just in case we should need them later. When Herman protested, Sherman spoke up and said (in his deep voice), "Yo, Herm. They were originally promised to me before our group even formed. While three of us are into sports, Jimmy is the one who's into music. I agree with Joe."

Personally, being that two of our original song ideas up to that point came primarily from me, all while teaching our group how to sing, when Joe handed me Delores' love notes to hold, I agreed to do so. For the record, when I looked over them a few days later, I found them to be very personal and emotional. For the most part, each was short and rhymed quite well. I could tell that some were written on the spur of the moment, whether typed or quickly written by hand. Undoubtedly, she was moved in her heart to pen truly poetic letters of love, seemingly to the same guy.

As it relates directly to the composition of *Why Do Fools Fall in Love*: When time permitted for me to do so at home, I looked over each poetic letter of love one by one. While they all had poetic words of love popping off the pages that were akin to the words of certain love songs out at the time, the words most often referred to feelings of "I Need You, I Want You, and I Love You." The one that caught my eye was titled "Why Do Birds Sing So Gay." That particular note had a different, imaginary, and catchy twist as Delores made her point of not being accepted and removed from the one she might have foolishly fallen in love with or was infatuated with. She literally felt that love was a losing game and asked the question, "Why?" Had she fallen for some guy, and the relationship failed or just didn't work? Perhaps due to his unavailability in her life, she was made to feel like she had made a fool of herself by falling for him with all her heart and love. Only then did she summarize that love was a losing game.

Mrs. Green seemingly wanted to release her disappointing love feelings without anyone knowing the specifics of how her love for someone affected her. Doing so with short love notes that disguised her feelings permitted her to do so without mentioning names. With her creative nature, she referenced how birds always sang together gayfully and wondered how they never departed—always together, even until the coming daylight. As many women do, Mrs. Green strongly expressed her true feelings beyond the joy of love, especially when feeling in her heart that she was foolishly taken advantage of by a man who was no longer "available."

As referenced earlier, that note included words from "Earth Angel" by The Penguins that aided her as she wrote, "I'm just a fool…a fool in love…with you." So importantly, around the time the four of us boys graduated from Stitt JHS, I took that typed poetic love note, "Why Do Birds Sing So Gay," and turned it into a slow 1-6-2-5 ballad that ultimately became *Why Do Fools Fall in Love*, which turned the music world around. Following are the words to that famous song:

"Why do birds sing so gay,
And lovers await the break of day?
Why do they fall in love?
Why does the rain fall from up above?
Why do fools fall in love?
Why do they fall in love?
Love is a losing game.
Love can be a shame.
I know of a fool, you see,
For that fool is me.
Tell me why…
Why do they fall in love?
Why does my heart skip this crazy beat?
For I know it will reach defeat.
So, tell me why…
Tell me why…
Why do fools fall in love?"

After showing the group my *Why Do Fools Fall in Love* slow song idea — inspired by Mrs. Green's "Why Do Birds Sing So Gay" terrific, original words — with Herman singing the lead initially, it became a beautiful ballad that we hoped to sing at summer talent shows. We also had two of my other original songs that MacDonald of The Capitols aided me in writing: "Please Be Mine" and "I Want You to Be My Girl." Both were sung at the Audubon Ballroom gathering near the end of June for the Stitt 9th-grade graduates. All those teens fell in love with our songs, especially the girls. I also kept my promise to Howard Jenkins (the lead singer of my first Stitt vocal group, "The Earth Angels") and brought him on to sing with us. By that time, we were popular in the neighborhood as The Ermines.

That June, our group's two original songs got huge applause from the girls. Similarly, we received the same level of loving attention at two Stitt summer talent shows the following month. Notably, while those two July 1955 talent shows gave The Ermines attention, the most remarkable phenomenon was that we had been given love notes, out of which one was on its way to becoming our first and greatest hit song, *Why Do Fools Fall in Love.*

So, with those very vital details in place regarding The Ermines and our three original songs, I can move on with my life story. The best is yet to come—when our fifth singer, Frankie Lymon, enters the picture. In fact, it highlights a critical stage in my life when the conclusion of my ultimate dream came into existence: global fame in 1956.

A PICTURE WALK THROUGH 1956-1957 MUSIC HISTORY

"Frankie Lymon and The Teenagers" (January 1956)
being promoted after their first recording: Joe
(baritone), Sherman (bass), Jimmy (1st tenor),
Herman (2nd tenor), and Frankie (lead singer).

"Frankie Lymon and The Teenagers"
Photoshoot, early 1956.

Jimmy and Frankie, February 1956.

The Cash Box

VOL. XVII—No. 30   APRIL 14, 1956

The Teenagers, current Gee Record sensations, who hit nationally with their first release, "Why Do Fools Fall In Love", are seen above going over the score of their next release, "I Want You To Be My Girl" and "I'm Not A Know It All". From left to right are Herman Santiago, Sherman Garnes, Joe Negroni, Jimmy Merchant, George Goldner, Frankie Lyman, and Joe Kolsky. Goldner and Kolsky are co-owners of Gee Records. Frankie Lyman, 13 year old lead voice, is also the writer of "Why Do Fools Fall In Love".

March 1956. Live performance at the
Brooklyn Paramount Theatre in
Downtown Brooklyn, New York.

April 1956. The group's major coast-to-coast TV show, "Live from Hollywood: Shower of Stars," with Frankie Laine (pictured), Joe E. Brown, Jane Russell, Nelson Riddle, and many others.

With Teen-Ager singing partners John Negroni (l.) and Herman Santiago, 14-year old Frankie Lymon chats with movie star Jane Russell before appearing on CBS television show. The youthful group's two other singers are Jimmy Merchant and Sherman Garnes.

A photo from the group's first of three
one-night city tours in 1956.
Each tour included roughly 60 one-nighter shows.

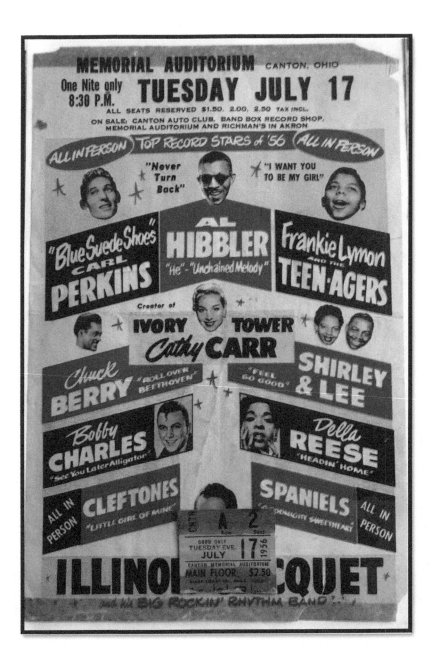

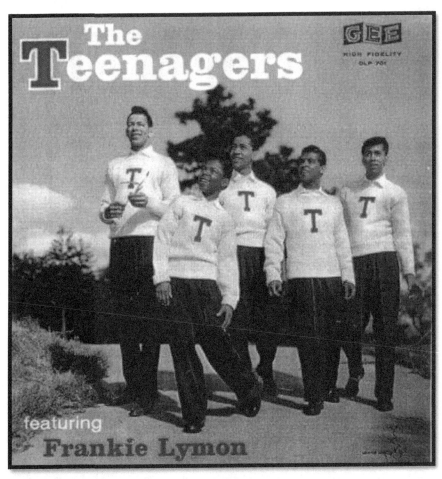

The group's 12-song LP. Released December 1956.

The group's first movie. January 1957.

Ten-day tour in Panama. March 1957.

Jimmy Merchant with "Teenagers" fans
during the Panama tour.

The group on tour in England, Ireland, and Scotland.
April through June 1957.

June 1957. The group's 2nd movie, "Mister Rock and Roll," and their last on-screen performance together as Frankie Lymon and The Teenagers.

Pencil sketch drawing of Elsie Merchant,
Jimmy's mother.

Pencil sketch drawing of Barbara Ann Merchant,
Jimmy's first wife *(deceased).*

Pencil sketch drawing of Mary Merchant,
Jimmy's wife of over 30 years.

CHAPTER 6: FRANKIE LYMON AND THE TEENAGERS – PART 1

In early August 1955, Frankie Lymon—a phenomenal 12-year-old singer whom both Sherman and Herman knew well and who lived in an apartment building next to Stitt JHS at 470 West 165th Street directly across the street from Herman—became key to our group's success. Frankie was born to Jeanette and Howard Lymon on September 30, 1942. His father was a truck driver and amateur singer who sang with a vocal group known as Harlem Aires. Frankie was the second of four boys: Howard Jr., Lewis, and Timothy, respectively. All were musically skilled, three of whom were made into a kid group by their dad that became known as The Esquires. In fact, the trio performed during one of the two Stitt talent shows where we sang as The Ermines the month before. During their performance, Howie played a Congo drum, Frankie played his bongos, and the other shook maracas. Interestingly, Frankie could sing R&B with a Latin feel at a young age.

Fun fact: In 1957, Lewis Lymon became a big music star as Lewis Lymon and The Teenchords. Years after Frankie's passing, Lewis sang with The Teenagers on occasion.

Much like all the Greater New York schools in the area in the early 1950s, Stitt had its share of amateur singers, especially 'group-wise.' At the time, songs that exploded onto the music scene on the radio, such as "Sixty-Minute Man," "Have Mercy, Baby," and "That's What You're Doing to Me" by The Dominoes were ones I showed my guys how to sing wherever and whenever we could. We regularly sang in our school's hallway (for the echo/acoustics) and on the street corners.

For the record, the birthdates of The Ermines members (oldest to youngest) are:

- Jimmy Merchant (me) – February 10, 1940
- Sherman Garnes – June 8, 1940
- Joe Negroni – September 9, 1940
- Herman Santiago – February 18, 1941

Frankie (born September 30, 1942) often watched us intently as we rehearsed at Stitt Night Center in preparation for our third talent show. Bobby Tesman of The Capitols and his lady friend, Lorraine Clark, also observed the 12-year-old boy easily slipping into our harmony and stage steps. He had a natural exuberance for show business with a charmed flair. He seemingly maturely saw himself as a high tenor voice in our background harmony and jumped into singing a duet with Herman on the song I had composed, "I Want You to Be My Girl." That day, Frankie demonstrated his natural abilities and that he was a possible pre-teen "kid" star. A few other child stars at the time included Teresa Brewer, Frank "Sugar Chile" Robinson, Little Esther, Tony Harper, and numerous gospel groups with pre-teen singers.

In talking with Frankie, Joe and I found him to be a know-it-all type of kid. He was the type of person who wanted to know everything about everything, all while being very enthusiastic concerning accomplishing his personal goals in life. Although his mom had four boys, she kept a particularly watchful eye over Frankie's fast-growing personality and character. I fondly remember him being a 12-year-old boy with boundless energy. Fortunately for us, Joe was able to keep Frankie in line, primarily because Frankie respected Joe's cool business and musical acumen.

When Frankie asked to join our group, the boldness of his request could not be overstated. After all, he was only twelve! After casually looking at Sherm, Joe, and Herm, I finally told Frankie we might be able to use him in our background. As part of his audition, I let him know we needed to test his lead voice by him singing "That's What You're Doing to Me" by The Dominoes. He knew the song well and held our undivided attention while effortlessly singing the tune. I then had him sing background with Joe, Sherman, and me on the original slow love song I had come up with from the love notes, "Why Do Birds Sing So Gay," with Herman as the lead singer. (At that point, the song had yet to be renamed *Why Do Fools Fall in Love*.) Frankie also picked up on that song easily as I showed him our smooth 1-6-2-5 soft love song harmony. We let him join us during the August Stitt talent show, singing The Dominoes' song.

During this time, I had Joe seriously consider changing our group's name from The Ermines. Collectively, we settled on the name "The Premiers."

Lorraine Clark saw in us a promising future in recording records and show business. Wanting to help us, she scheduled a meeting for Joe and me to visit her. At the meeting, she explained to us all the amazing possibilities that she desired on our behalf. We could tell she had a genuine passion for seeing us succeed after hearing and watching our group perform and even moreso after observing our Stitt rehearsal with Frankie.

Although Lorraine was unable to keep her promise of taking our group to the Apollo Theatre to see The Penguins of "Earth Angel" fame (for reasons unknown), she managed to get us an interview with a radio DJ in an office located just above the Apollo marquee. After our short interview, we decided to sing the song that the five of us did so well (with Frankie singing lead), "That's What You're Doing to Me." After doing so, the five of us were floored by our live, on-air performance, which truly showed our advancement in the musical arena.

Being all the more impressed, Lorraine then took us to compete at one of the Apollo Amateur Night talent shows. That night, a wheelchair singer received an outstanding ovation and won the contest. Although we performed well again while singing "That's What You're Doing to Me" by The Dominoes (with Frankie singing lead), the overall experience in a packed house of screaming admirers at that great theatre was truly unforgettable. I cannot fail to mention here that Chuck Berry performed that night as well, which is noteworthy because we were unaware that we would one day soon work with him.

On the first Saturday in September, Lorraine arranged to have us perform at the PS143 JHS Amateur Talent Show. The well-known group The

Cadillacs were special guests, and their lead singer, 'Speedo,' encouraged our group to make records. (We had no idea that The Cadillacs would be on a show with us when we became famous like them.) Joe and I were even more startled and further encouraged by Speedo's words.

I pause here to recall the first time we signed autographs, and Sherman changed our group name from The Premiers to The Coup De Villes.

Interestingly, during that time at the beginning of our musical career, Lorraine and Richard Barrett of The Valentines became acquainted with one another. Both were interested in our group in a big way, particularly after Frankie joined us and sang with us on stage at Stitt's talent show that August. Like us, Richard's vocal group also rehearsed at Stitt. While he was a fabulous group performer, it was he who became a key figure in our group's lives after he discovered us and then set up our audition at Gee Records with its owner, Mr. George Goldner.

♫ ♫ ♫ ♫ ♫

Richard Barrett—whose group, The Valentines, had recorded "Lily Maebelle" on Goldner's Rama

Records label—was thrilled about getting us five boys to George's office to meet him at Gee Records.

Joe looked at each of us and said excitedly, "Do you hear that, guys?"

"Yeah, man," Sherman replied in his classic deep voice.

Frankie's joy was likely unmatched at that moment. "C'mon, guys! He knows what he's doing!"

"We'll see," responded Herman. As the quiet one in the group, that lackadaisical response was expected from him.

As for me, I smiled broadly as I thought to myself, "Wow! My dream is really moving forward and coming to pass!" The dream phenomenon was so significant in my life. For as long as I can remember, I only wanted to sing and be a part of a vocal group. Without even realizing it, I was already a fantastic music instructor who could build perfect harmonies with ease. Just the thought of recording in a studio was a major turn-on, especially since Frankie had come into the group as our background singer.

Before taking us to meet Goldner, Richard invited us to his apartment to give us some background and what to expect during the discussion. He explained that George's company was actually a Latin brand and that George was one of the guys that started Latin music with Tico Records. He then moved into the R&B music industry with a company called Gee Records and recorded two groups. Richard encouraged us by saying, "Although Mr. Goldner is still interested in producing Latin groups, because you guys have two Puerto Ricans in your group, that should appeal to him." It remains interesting to me that George was a clean-cut Jew handling those different genres of music.

George Goldner's office was downtown at 220 West 42nd Street. The five of us boys took the subway to meet him and Richard at what was Tico Records at the time. George was seated at his desk and got right down to business. "Let me hear you guys sing," he said. We presented a couple of Rock 'n' Roll songs, with Joe and Herman taking turns singing the lead. "Who else sings lead in the group?" he asked.

I replied, "Well, Mr. Goldner, that's basically it. Joe and Herman."

"What about that little kid back there?" George asked.

Frankie quickly stepped from behind Sherman and asked, "Are you talking about me, Mr. Goldner?"

"Yes. I'm talking about you, little boy."

"Don't call me 'little boy.' My name is Frankie!"

Obviously surprised by the fire in the response, George replied, "Oh. Okay, Frankie. You're right. We all want to be called by our name."

"That's right, Mr. Goldner," Frankie said with a smile. "Now, what do you want?"

"What do you do?"

"I sing background. You heard me singing background with the other guys."

"Yes, I did, but can you sing any lead songs?"

Frankie's boldness showed up again. "Mr. Goldner, what do you want to hear? I sing them all!"

"Is there anything you can sing with the group?"

"Yes. There's one I sang with them at a couple of talent shows."

"Okay, Frankie. Let me hear it." The five of us sang "That's What You're Doing to Me" by The Dominoes for George. Before we could complete the first two choruses, he said, "Mr. Barrett, I want you to work with these boys." He then turned to us and said, "By the way, boys, Frankie is the new lead singer of your group. Come back and see me in two weeks."

We left the meeting that day feeling elated. We couldn't believe we were going to actually record for a real label…until Richard reminded us of one thing: "Guys, what do you think you're going to be recording? Other groups' songs? You need original material."

"How can we record our originals? Frankie doesn't sing them," I stated.

Richard's response was direct: "You gotta let Frankie learn them."

So, I started breaking Frankie in with the three songs we had since the inception of The Ermines/The Premiers/The Coup De Villes: "Please Be Mine," "I Want You to Be My Girl," and "Why Do Birds Sing So

Gay." I also let him know the title of the latter would be changed to *Why Do Fools Fall in Love.*

While Richard Barrett agreed to the name change, he also suggested the song be converted to a more up-tempo one—which was a transition we made. The song was all ready to go with its new flow by the time we returned to the studio to record *Why Do Fools Fall in Love* on December 3, 1955.

♫ ♫ ♫ ♫ ♫

A fond, funny memory I have of those days is when Richard Barrett (a barber by trade) wanted to prepare The Teenagers for our stage presence. He took the four of us to his apartment and showed us how he did his own hair (he had a style called Marcel, similar to what is known today as finger waves but with a looser flow). To give you an idea of what the Marcel hairdo looked like on men, envision people such as Little Richard, Billy Eckstine, Jackie Robinson, and Sugar Ray Robinson—to name a few.

When Richard pulled out this white stuff in a jar, he instructed Sherman to take a seat. He then began putting the stuff in Sherman's hair, all while the rest of us stared in bewilderment. The next thing we knew,

Sherman started screaming, "It's burning! It's burning!"

Richard replied, "Hold on, Sherman. Let me straighten and comb it through some more!"

"No, man! Get this stuff out of my hair! It's burning!" Sherman yelled.

Richard took him to the sink, rinsed it out, and boom! Sherman had straight hair! He then gestured for me to sit and get the stuff put in my hair.

"Me?" I asked. "You want ME to get THAT in my hair?!"

Herman chimed in, "Look at my hair. I want my hair straight like his, too!"

"Herman, your hair's already straight enough. Jimmy, sit down!" Richard stated.

As you can imagine, I was uneasy about the process after witnessing what Sherman endured with his burning head incident. Meanwhile, Sherman was in the mirror, combing through his new, slick hair. Before doing my hair, Richard said, "Jimmy, watch what I do to Sherman's hair." With expertise, he waved Sherman's slick hairdo and then tied it up with a scarf.

"Why are you tying his hair up with a scarf? He looks like a woman!" I teased.

Richard's response was very matter-of-fact: "Well, get used to looking like a woman. All of you. Now, Jimmy, come sit and get your hair done!" After the white stuff was put in my hair, I started screaming about the burn almost immediately, but Richard said, "No, Jimmy. Your hair is a bit rougher than Sherman's. I need to put in a bit more work on you." Admittedly, my hair was knottier than Sherman's and not so "easy" to handle. Once the stuff was removed, he waved my hair. However, the style didn't last long because we lacked the passion and ability for upkeep.

Notably, most Black groups at the time had a Marcel. I remember getting on the bus after performing on tour and how we quickly put on our scarves to protect our hair.

♫♫♫♫♫

In sharing the history of The Teenagers' time with Frankie Lymon, I need to highlight details concerning our music's recording and release dates and the blatant, criminal misuse of names credited regarding songwriters. Before going any further, I must share that Goldner was affiliated with big brass people in the mob world, including Morris Levy, who loaned money to Goldner.

Why Do Fools Fall in Love and its flipside, *Please Be Mine*, were both written by me: Jimmy Merchant. Both songs were recorded in the studio on December 3, 1955. As referenced before, when the "Fools" was initially released, the writers were listed as Lymon-Santiago-Goldner but were changed shortly after to just Lymon-Goldner. Ironically, the adults in the room—Richard Barrett, Morris Levy, and George Goldner—were in the studio when "Fools" was recorded. Sadly, they proved to be dishonest men by essentially 'stealing' the rights for the music from us—the songwriters.

In February 1956, our group recorded "Love Is a Clown" (written by Goldner's wife) and "Am I Fooling Myself Again," a smooth mid-tempo song. "I Want You to Be My Girl" (that I came up with) and its flipside, "I'm Not a Know-It-All" (written by two White songwriters), were also recorded around the 16th of February. When "Fools" became a hit song, other artists approached us, wanting us to record their songs to help them gain notoriety in the music business. "I Want You to Be My Girl" (as stated, it was a song I wrote that Richard Barrett put his name on as the writer) was Frankie Lymon and The Teenagers' second release and was another huge hit.

In May 1956, we recorded "Who Can Explain" (written by Abner Silver and Roy Alfred). Although it was never released, it was intended to be an actual response to the question, "Why do fools fall in love?" On May 15th, we recorded "ABCs of Love" (Levy and Barrett were listed as the writers) and "I Promise to Remember," written by Jimmy Castor and Jimmy Smith.

In August 1956, "ABCs of Love" and "Share" were released on radio. That same month, "I'm Not a Juvenile Delinquent" and "Baby, Baby" were recorded for a movie we starred in called *Rock, Rock, Rock*.

In October 1956, we recorded "Paper Castles" and "Teenage Love" — a song that was written by a gay guy I went to school with who kept knocking on my door, insisting that our group sing his song. His name was Al Cooper. Once again, Levy put his name on that song exclusively, as well as our "Juvenile Delinquent" tune.

In February 1957, we recorded "Fortunate Fellow," "Love Put Me Out of My Head," and "Out in the Cold Again" with Frankie. When the song was released, "Out in the Cold's" flipside was "Miracle in the Rain." An interesting tidbit here is that while on tour in England that year, a classmate wrote me a letter asking why only Frankie's name was listed on "Miracle in the Rain." It was then that I began to notice that after three 60-day 1956 U.S. tours, theaters, and TV shows, our managers were in the beginning stages of breaking apart our vocal group. Our departure from the U.S. to tour overseas was when everything started to fall apart, and we were accompanied by people who were part of the plan to separate our group.

During our trip to England, the Queen wanted to see us perform after a recommendation from The Platters, who had also performed for her. Much to our surprise, she was already familiar with us from "Fools" and our group being called "The Rage of the Age" in that country after we hit the #1 spot on the music charts in London—the very first time an American song hit that pinnacle of greatness in England! It was apparent we had made it to the 'Big Time,' but what mattered to our management was Frankie Lymon.

While in England, we were out-of-control boys who got kicked out of the best hotels during our first week there because many teen girl "visitors" came to our room. It must be mentioned that our road manager at the time allowed our rowdy behavior. As I'm sure you can imagine, he was fired and sent back to the U.S. In his place, we were given a strict schoolteacher to serve as our overseer, along with a more business-minded road manager.

Once we managed to calm down there and got our act together, Frankie Lymon and The Teenagers recorded and released five additional songs: "Together," "You," "It Would Be So Nice," "Fortunate Fellow," and "I Was Alone." The Teenagers weren't listed on any of those titles.

Back in the states, in May 1957, we recorded "Begin the Beguine" — a song written by Cole Porter that we redid with Sherman singing the bass lead — and "You Can't Be True." Those were the last songs The Teenagers recorded with Frankie before he took on a solo singing career.

An interesting note is that after the group separated, Joe Negroni started managing women. One of them became a legitimate actress whose name was Darby Lloyd Rains. Darby was first a vocal group singer for Joe, who became his girlfriend. In the 1970s, she became an adult film star, a fact that is public knowledge.

CHAPTER 7: FRANKIE LYMON AND THE TEENAGERS – PART 2

The New York Times published a first-page write-up about Frankie Lymon and The Teenagers dated Thursday, November 19, 1992 – 37 years after *Why Do Fools Fall in Love* was recorded. The article was posted directly under two large photos of President-Elect Bill Clinton, with President George Bush greeting him. The other photo was of Mr. Clinton with a female congresswoman. The write-up was written as follows:

Title: **"Here's Who First Asked the Big Question: Why Do Fools Fall in Love?"**

"It was 1955. There was a revolution on the radio, and five kids from Washington Heights signed up as foot soldiers just after the birth of Rock 'n Roll. They had their moment. That moment was a simple, tender song called 'Why Do Fools Fall in Love.' The group was Frankie Lymon and The Teenagers. For nearly 40 years, as the song was recorded and re-recorded into the pop music tandem, the boy with the sweet soprano and that first blockbuster hit were joined in Rock 'n Roll immortality."

Wow, folks! You can see what *Why Do Fools Fall in Love* did for the music industry. Historically speaking, that write-up was in light of the songwriters' rights court case with the only other original Teenager, Herman, and me. (We won that case, by the way.)

Other articles were published about our group's fame and popularity, but only after the song was abused, misused, and stolen. Another write-up in the New York Times of particular note pertained to the court ruling just before our group was inducted into the Rock 'n Roll Hall of Fame, and I'll share it here:

Title: **"Taken for a Spin in the Song Business: The Hijacking of a Rock 'n Roll Record."**

"In mid-November, amid a presidential campaign turned ugly, a stagnant economy, and world turmoil, America was a country in the mood for some good news — a clear-cut case of right and wrong, where the good news guys win. As if scripted to order, such an item came across the wire. A federal judge in New York had ruled that Jimmy Merchant and Herman Santiago — two of the original members of '50s Doo-Wop pioneers, Frankie Lymon and The Teenagers — who cowrote the group's 1956 classic, Why Do Fools Fall in Love, were entitled to royalties. The judge agreed with Carl E. Person (the lawyer representing Merchant and Santiago), who claimed the late George Goldner (former president of Gee Records) had incorrectly filed the copyright of the song when he listed the writers as Lymon and himself. Person pointed out that his clients had

been paid no royalties for 38 years. Estimated, they could now receive at least $4 million. This was a news director's dream, and it played on local and national broadcasts for days after the November 17th ruling."

I believe it was imperative that I paint that picture for the readers of our group's great history before getting into the meat of this chapter. Moving forward, what you will read speaks of what occurred once our group sang our way to international fame.

♫ ♫ ♫ ♫ ♫

Frankie Lymon and The Teenagers are a great part of American music history and cornerstones of Rock 'n Roll. Our group is primarily responsible for the beginnings of the kiddie vocal group craze. I do not find it robbery to say we are critical to the youth movement in music from 1956 to this very day.

Throughout 1956 into mid-1957, our group worked with older, seasoned entertainers, and we even closed shows after their performances. In the Philadelphia Tribune, one writer said, "They [Frankie Lymon and The Teenagers] have swept the nation overnight and are currently drawing raves and claims from critics from coast to coast as the nation's newest hit sensation." Sentiments like that were written time and again by various writers. We, of course, were beyond that of many young boys who got together in other big cities. In most cases, their flame died, and their groups disbanded—but our future looked assured!

The youth vocal group craze commonly began in schools. In fact, that is the root of our group's story. When "Fools" was on its way to selling 100,000 copies in the first three weeks, it was apparent it had become an instant hit among youth and adults alike. A fun fact is that the song remained on the record charts for six months before becoming an international hit overseas, where it was released on red and gold Gee Record labels, pressed and distributed by Columbia Records as "The Teenagers featuring Frankie Lymon." In England, they didn't view Frankie as more significant than The Teenagers. Instead, they viewed The Teenagers as the actual power of the group. Of course, Frankie wasn't less than any of us; it was just how that country made us appear.

Back to the first week of January 1956: With Why Do Fools Fall in Love powering the market and the four of us 10th-graders walking the halls of school (Frankie was only in 8th grade at the time), I recall the time I was changing classes, and there was a girl heading to the same class. She was a young White girl, and she was singing, "Tell me whyyyy…" — the hook of "Fools." I loved the idea that a girl was singing the song, but I couldn't figure out how she had heard it so quickly. After all, Mr. Goldner said it wasn't going to be released until the beginning of January! Apparently, the radio stations began playing the song immediately upon receipt. (I had yet to hear it for myself at the time.) After the girl told me she heard the song on the radio, I was surprised to learn that even White stations were playing it! On the way home from school that day, I rushed home and tried to find the song on the radio.

♫ ♫ ♫ ♫ ♫

After Sherman, Joe, Herman, and I met and then went together to Frankie's building, we talked about the superstars we might become. We were all excited about the mere possibility of becoming famous! We had heard people talking about the record and realized we were on our way to working, performing, and having fun as true musical celebrities. Frankie and Joe knew it beyond a shadow of a doubt. The other three of us were aware of the potential but were hesitant to believe it would happen for us like the adult superstars. Nonetheless, we were all overjoyed by the possibility of fame.

Our first professional gig was at the State Theatre in Hartford, Connecticut, the weekend of February 11-12, 1956. The write-up advertising the event read as follows:

"An all-new Rock 'n Roll review will be featured at the State Theatre Saturday and Sunday. Headlining the company of 60 noted stars will be The Bonnie Sisters who skyrocketed to fame with their hit recording Crybaby. Co-headliners will be Bo Diddley, a popular Rock 'n Roll personality; The Cadillacs, singing Speedo; The Turbans, recording artists of When You Dance; The Harptones of Life is But a Dream fame; Jesse Powell and his 16-Month Rock 'n Roll band; and The Teenagers with Frankie Lymon, offering Why Do Fools Fall in Love. Performances will be continuous on both days, with the late stage shows nightly at 10:00 p.m."

It was an amazing weekend! Many memories were made, and we actually got paid! We also did dance hops and live interviews on the weekends, even beyond February. During those events, we would go on stage and perform, dancing and lip-singing. Our group was very busy on the weekends and sometimes after school.

Whenever we performed live, countless people came to see us. I'll be the first to say we had a certain intangible quality, partly because of our song's lyrics and harmony, but also because of our lead singer's voice that even made the whole greater than all five parts that played in our song. The music we produced wasn't just mere songs; they were all-encompassing, leading to something new in the music industry — the youth movement! Someone once said, *"They hit a bullseye every time."* Another said, *"More than mere songs, they welded a bond between us, our friends, and others of our generation in the same way mystical handshakes and code words help to bind members of secret societies. Here at last is music of our own. That's what it means for me to see Frankie up there on the stage. He represents me, my friends, and our entire generation, singing about things only we could relate to and in a style only we could understand."*

Wow!!! The compliments and feedback we constantly received were remarkable! We were on our way!

In no time, teens became the largest group of buyers of single records. At the time, virtually no Rock 'n Roll was available on long-playing records, which was why an album comprised of 12 of our songs was released on Gee Records at the end of 1956. The parents of youngsters purchased our album without hesitation. While teenagers loved R&B music, they could not identify with any negative messages related to drinking, failed relationships, and despair. Ironically, White teens comprised a significant portion of sales of our records and even moreso seats at our shows. Perhaps it was because "Fools" was not ethnic, coupled with our lead's voice being sensual with no sexual hidden agenda. It was an honor to be a part of a group that fueled the dreams of countless other would-be stars.

♫ ♫ ♫ ♫ ♫

"Fools" sold very strongly, well into May 1956. Although we were all overjoyed about our fame and making money (often $3,500 or more per gig), we were still teenagers stumbling our way through life. I recall one lesson in particular: learning how to play on beautiful girls (mainly White), despite being watched over by our road manager, Charlie Lavigne, who was hired by George Goldner. Charlie cared for us, all while knowing we (as boys) attracted girls to our hotel rooms like the older performers did after shows. As for me, I accumulated a list of girls, even having sex with the ones I liked. I remember the time when Zola Taylor of The Platters asked which one of us would like to have sex with her. I "volunteered." As I left her hotel room that night to return to my own, I noticed

Frankie and The Platters' piano player, Ruppert Brinker, were there, watching us the whole time. Shocking, I know...

In terms of wisdom, some of the older performers kept an eye on us while on the road, including Clyde McPhatter and Vicky Burgess of The Joytones, whom I got to know very well. In fact, we became close during our first show at the Apollo Theatre. In 1958, she became the mother of my first daughter, Victoria. I remember once how, between shows, we were rushed downtown to appear live on the Jerry Lewis Telethon for Cerebral Palsy at Madison Square Garden. We went on just before Sammie Davis, Jr. and was then rushed right back to the Apollo. Before departing the telethon, Mr. Davis spoke the following uplifting words to us: "I don't know if I can follow you, boys. You guys did a great job. Keep up the good work."

On the road, our group did phenomenal interviews, even while having to go to southern states where racial hatred was the most profound. We witnessed White men picketing and protesting, objecting to Black shows in certain southern cities. There was also a group of younger Black and White boys and girls with their own signs, following the protesters. Their signs read, **"ROCK 'N ROLL IS**

HERE TO STAY!" —and they repeated those words loudly over the racist protesters. It must be noted that some of the youths were younger than our group.

Even at one of our southern performances on tour, they had removed the stage curtain from behind us and seated all the Black people in that area. All the performers were instructed to face and sing exclusively to the White crowd, but Frankie turned to face the Black audience. We followed his lead, all while wondering if we would end up getting shot in the back. The older performers told us not to be afraid, though.

The prejudice at that time was outright blatant. Regardless, Frankie was a kid who did what he felt was the right thing to do. We had to give credit where credit was due. Frankie was truly a star!

CHAPTER 8: THE DARK YEARS – PART 1

 While my vocal group's 1956 first hit song, *Why Do Fools Fall in Love*, is the key to my dream—an extraordinary musical legacy— it's the lessons learned along the way that made my life story worth sharing. Overall, I've learned that our lives are tools of God and that He brings things into our lives to be used by Him to benefit others when we become Christians.

Long before that realization, thoughts of writing my autobiography came to me at age 29 on Sunday, December 14, 1969, after seeing the first performance of the Jackson 5 on TV while in jail. At that moment, I found myself reminiscing on the days when Frankie Lymon and The Teenagers were "IT"—the start of the youth movement of kid-singing groups.

I battled many dark years after the group's breakup. Some of those details will now follow, but I must forewarn you: Some of the information shared here is not for young audiences.

♫ ♫ ♫ ♫ ♫

Unfortunately, all the dreams of each of us five boys to do great things musically suddenly went sour when Frankie Lymon was separated from us to become a solo artist. Notably, he was a 13-year-old, very cocky kid who was very bright and extremely talented. There's no denying: That boy could sing! He had a sort of high gospel voice with remarkable clarity. Aside from the uneasiness in Joe's life (our group's leader), all hell broke loose in the rest of our lives. Sherman, Herman, Frankie, and I spun into what seemed like perpetual darkness as street-life habitual drug users. A lot of the history is far too much to cover in this book, but I will share more than enough to demonstrate just how lost and broken we were.

Personally, I began looking for ways to cope with my new reality on the streets, even while still singing. I needed to make money, so I resorted to selling drugs during the period of my life that I refer to as **'The Dark Years'** (1958 to 1980). Sadly, those years also encompass the loss of my darling first wife, Barbara, whose life I take full responsibility for when she passed away in the hospital. Even today, in terms of what she endured, those thoughts flood my mind from time to time. However, I do thank God for how He used me to lead her to accept Jesus as her personal Lord and Savior before her passing, and so with her mother. So, as you may see, even as I write my story at the age of 83, there are unfortunate life experiences that occurred during those dark years that I must share leading up to the end of my 'Part One' autobiographical work.

♫ ♫ ♫ ♫ ♫

Now, getting back to when I first decided to write a book about my fame and the 1968 unfortunate and untimely death of Frankie Lymon at age 25...

When I saw the first performance of the Jackson 5 on TV, I was doing a six-month bid in jail at Rikers Island Prison (October 4, 1969 - March 28, 1970). The charge was 'Breaking and Entering.' Another dope addict and I broke into a small grocery store through the back window in the middle of the night to steal cases of beer to sell on the street, along with other "valuables." The day I was sentenced, my first wife, one of our children, my mom, my oldest sister Gert, and my Teenager buddy Sherman all sat in the courtroom with sad eyes as the judge stated my fate.

Coincidently, during my first week in jail, I was blown away when I saw Teenager Herman Santiago there. At the time, we were both in line to get breakfast but on opposite sides of the prison mess hall. When he saw me, he remained cool as always. I learned he was in jail for drug-related charges, too. In fact, he was nearly finishing up a 90-day bid. As we talked, he

137

shared with me that the dorm he was in housed singers and musicians, which prompted me to request a transfer to his dorm. Herman was, in fact, playing the clarinet for the jail's band and made daily trips to the jail's studio (the clarinet was the instrument he got interested in after first seeing Sherman play the saxophone and me the trumpet while attending Stitt JHS). Then, out of the clear blue, Sherman popped up. He received 60 days for some kind of check forgery to, of course, get money for drugs.

Three members of The Teenagers in jail 'doing time' at the same time still rocks my thoughts.

Shortly after connecting with Sherman behind bars, he also switched over to the musician's dorm to occupy his time by playing the saxophone. There was another vocal group singer we knew named James Stanley, who also attended Stitt JHS. We learned he received a one-year sentence. When the four of us hooked up, we began singing as a vocal group aided by a skilled older musician known as Shafi Hadi. Shafi taught us how to sing jazz music arrangements. A few other well-known musicians were there, including Charlie Mingus and Hank Mobley. While in Rikers, Shafi managed to get Sherman, Herman, James, and me to become a great jazz vocal group, singing like my two favorite groups: The Four Freshmen and The Hi-

Los. That same man taught us a great top-flight arrangement of the song "Girl Talk" that blew away all the prison cats who observed us. However, no matter how "enjoyable" music made our time in the joint, the four of us failed to change our lives when we were released. Our affiliation with the streets as "dope-world dudes" (in our minds) anxiously waited for us just outside of Rikers' doors.

In fact, the four of us—Sherman, Herman, James, and I—tried putting together a vocal group that didn't work out due to Sherman leaving. I then encountered a known lead singer named Butchie Saunders of The Elchords, whose hit song was Peppermint Stick. I felt we had a chance because he could easily copy Frankie Lymon's style. There was also a woman in the music business that truly wanted to manage us after also taking pictures. When that arrangement didn't work, we fell apart...again. Sadly, James Stanley disappeared shortly after (rumor has it he was supposedly 'taken out' (killed) by some Jersey boys due to James misusing their money). As for Sherman, he had medical issues but was still strung out on dope. A few years after I tried to get him to sing with Herman, James, and me, he passed away on February 26, 1977. His funeral service was a truly sad day in the lives of Herman, Joe, and me.

A sidenote regarding an important historic time with Joe: After reviewing our group's crushing downfall and Frankie and Sherman's deaths, Joe and I discussed writing books that we both had in mind. When I told him my plans and that I still wanted to sing whenever I got my head together, he agreed and then made a comment about Herman. Basically, he stated that even though Herman and I tried forming a new group with Sherman and James in the early '70s, using a female manager, I was different from Herman. He added that although it didn't work out due to our drug-use lives, I was always more energetic than Herman about getting things done. Then, when I referenced the key importance of our group's strength—that being two original Teenagers came first—although Joe agreed with me, he replied, "That reality would never work." I couldn't understand how Joe could speak so negatively about Herman, his Puerto Rican buddy that started The Teenagers with him. He emphasized that, from a business standpoint, there were notable differences between Herman and me and that he and Herman would always be friends regardless. Joe then added, "You're the person who moves and gets things done, on and off the stage." Perhaps that is the reason Herman and I looked down on each other later in life.

In response, all I could say was, "Wow."

Still, rather than write a book or get back on stage once I left Rikers Island Prison, I returned to the craziness of the street world.

Incidentally, Joe was also housing trunks of marijuana and cocaine for a high-powered buddy at the time. He told me, "If you need money, I'll be glad to give you packages of this stuff to sell for me." I didn't need to be coaxed into it. I immediately jumped on Joe's offer. After I started selling, a younger cousin of my wife Barbara stole two dozen of the $5.00 bags of weed I had stashed away while visiting us.

Then, when I became known as a street dope dealer, two plainclothes cops came into the pool room where I hung out, took me into the hallway of the building next door, and searched all my pockets—all while instructing me to take off my clothes. When they found nothing, they still took me to jail overnight. When I went to court the following day, the judge immediately released me.

♫ ♫ ♫ ♫ ♫

Now, to get into the very important legal aspect of music: A song lives two lives simultaneously. While it is, of course, personal property, it's also an emotional soundtrack that affects the lives of those who purchase that recording based on their love of music. In the '50s, we called it 'buying a record to play on the record player' (that was long before CDs and streaming music). Any time or anywhere any song is played, heard, and enjoyed worldwide, whoever owns the copyright and/or wrote it is paid royalties (a percentage of each record sold globally). At times, however, the actual songwriter does not legally own its copyright and cannot be paid royalties every time their song is played on the radio, sold in record shops, or performed in a movie or TV special.

With that said, had our vocal group's parents been made aware of those music recording professional legalities at the start of our singing careers, we—Frankie Lymon and The Teenagers—would be financially secure for the remainder of our days. A financial legacy could be left for our families after our deaths because they would constantly receive our songwriters' royalties (four times a year), along with our performance royalties (from seven two-sided hit records) and others.

Regarding our parents and concerning the songwriting royalties we never received: It was no fault of theirs. I'm talking about the millions of dollars earned over the past 70 years, especially from our biggest hit song, *Why Do Fools Fall in Love*. When George Goldner chose to use his and Frankie's name as the sole contributors of the song (after outright lying to us regarding the use of names on the label), he used the opportunity to move his way into owning 50% of our music. I later came to learn that it was commonplace at the time for record producers to "steal" from their artists that way. Countless artists were ripped off for their royalties, including The Teenagers, all while Goldner wisely promoted Frankie as our group's key songwriter and child star. I clearly recall the round red paper record labels printed up that read, *Why Do Fools Fall in Love:* **Lymon, Santiago, and Goldner**. On the flip side, *Please Be Mine* read the same (that was the ballad I wrote and for which I have a so-called songwriter's contract).

The next startling absolute lie from George Goldner came after the first pressing of thousands of records sold in records stores were the names printed on the record labels: Lymon and Goldner — only, purposefully removing Herman's last name. We all flipped out when we saw Goldner's name next to Frankie's on both the 78 and 45 record labels. While Goldner said he was entitled to a share of our royalties, he added, "Frankie's name is there to strengthen your group's recognition," assuring that all five of us would get equal royalty shares of the remaining 50 percent. When Frankie separated from us in mid-'57, that 50% share of our songs went with him and continues to be sent to his family today. Regarding the other 50% that went to Golder, I cannot fail to mention that he is basically responsible for our group's superstardom (record-wise) while turning out to also be our songwriters' royalties thief. Overall, while Goldner was largely into making money for himself, he did so while selling us brilliantly — leading me to believe (as I write these words) that he wasn't fully responsible for moving Frankie from us into a solo artist. Still, it is evident Goldner couldn't care less about the young (and old) lives he negatively impacted along the way.

♫♫♫♫♫

If you believe as I do, you know that everything in life begins somewhere. Unfortunately, my group's terrible rip-off of our royalties began with a man from Philadelphia, Pennsylvania named Richard Barrett who discovered us in August 1955 (as previously mentioned). There is no doubt he was fully aware that the three songs he approached Goldner with were ours, long before taking us to Gee Records to be auditioned by Goldner. Much to my disappointment, all these years later, I recognize that Barrett is responsible for our group being ripped off for our songwriters' royalties, even as he operated in the position of our group's road manager.

The following is a very brief, important note concerning those two men from a February 1991 extensive New Yorker magazine write-up about Frankie Lymon and The Teenagers. George Goldner had moved into R&B from Latin music and was known in the business as both a 'very good promoter' and a 'bad gambling horse player.' In the article, Barrett is quoted as saying, *"I think in my heart, if he [Goldner] hadn't gambled, he wouldn't have shorted anybody, but everybody shorts somebody."*

Simply put: Richard Barrett—who **knew** the business—should have advised our parents wisely concerning the importance of getting a professional music attorney for their young sons after he got us a record deal with George Goldner. There was no way our families would have agreed to the arrangement had Barrett not shown himself to be business-smart concerning us entertainers and our royalty payments. At certain times later in life, he proved to be a fast talker with hustling know-how. Yes, he aided vocal groups tremendously, but he was arrogant and quickly grew into looking out for himself— *financially*. It saddens me as I think about him and write these words.

Many years later, concerning the "Why Do Fools Fall in Love" movie that was produced in 1998, Barrett invited Herman and me to his house out of state to discuss "a movie idea introduced to him regarding our group's history" that he wanted us to accept for practically less than nothing (financially). Herman and I both felt humiliated, thinking he would finally do something for us, but no. When he handed us a contract to sign for the movie, we refused. Disappointingly, the movie was all about Frankie Lymon's life, not the whole group.

Richard Barrett made his intent well-known when he placed his name on our second hit record, *I Want You to Be My Girl* (a song I wrote before Frankie joined the group), as one of its writers along with George Goldner. He was a royalty thief who teamed up with Goldner to "rob us blind." In fact, Barrett was listed as the co-writer of the last two songs that we, The Teenagers, were told by Goldner to record behind Frankie Lymon's lead singing 'solo track' after we were separated from him. Those two songs were *Love Put Me Out of My Head* and *Fortunate Fellow*. Both were made for the second Alan Freed movie, "Mr. Rock 'n Roll," that opened October 10, 1957, at the Lowe's Theatre on Broadway — four months after our group was divided. That was yet another instance of our group never receiving credit (royalty-wise). It's apparent that the two of them gave no thought regarding the sad loss of our writers' rights, along with our group's break-up pain while in England. While credited with our group's beginning, we were crushed by them. To this day, our families are penniless as it relates to our stolen writers' royalties that none of us four original members legally received.

As you can likely imagine, my childhood dream led to great discouragement. Nonetheless, our dear parents are clear of any blame, as they were unaware of what Goldner and Barrett were doing financially in their sons' lives. After all, they had no knowledge of what the music royalty income business was all about in both the short- and long-term scenarios.

♫ ♫ ♫ ♫ ♫

Sherman, Herman, Joe, and I learned more and more about our group's music royalty information and thievery from other well-known show business performers. Soon after, we also began to see our royalty trust funds mixed up in the same chaos. Along with our songwriters' stolen income, our overall earned performance monies were basically zero — the same as our singers' royalties from our Gee Record recordings. We later learned Morris Levy was the one collecting our Why Do Fools Fall in Love songwriters' royalties. How did that happen, you ask? Well, the 50% that Goldner credited to himself (stole) was signed over to the Roulette Records owner, Morris Levy, to pay off his large gambling debts.

I believe that misuse of power would have never happened if Richard Barrett had simply thought honestly and caringly of us five boys in the beginning when first seeing our potential and, of course, when "Fools" was released. Surely, he was perceptive concerning our prospective income! In fact, according to my notes, we earned over $256,000 in our first year by December 1956 via personal appearances countrywide, U.S. and foreign record royalties from Broadcast Music, Inc. (BMI), and songwriters' royalties. Overall, our entire vocal group earnings were called "trust funds," to be released to us when we turned 21. Before then, we had a new lead singer, Billy Lubrano (whom I will reference), who officially signed with us in October 1957.

The following year, I got busted and went to jail in March 1958, right before The Teenagers were scheduled to leave New York City on the 5th of April to work a 16-day, coast-to-coast itinerary with the famous solo singer, Mr. Roy Hamilton. I was jailed after being fingerprinted and having my mugshots taken the following morning due to being in a stolen car with two older dudes. I recall them giving the cops a hard time when the car we were in was blocked in Jamaica Queens by four police cars, just blocks from where I lived. That occurred when I was trying my best to be very positive about The Teenagers still performing regularly under the management of Al Joyner, the gentleman who began as our road manager while in Europe with Frankie. Mr. Joyner also knew my father and played poker games with him while he managed boxers. Mr. Joyner also managed two White teenage girl singers called "The Baby Dolls." One was Cathy, and the other, Roe Casalino, who, in July 1957, was from the Forest Hills area of Queens, New York, and steered me to our new lead singer, Billy Lubrano.

Up to that point, I used to only drink beer, smoke a little marijuana, and hosted small gatherings in the house of my family in Jamaica, Queens. I had yet to realize what street life was all about but often played pool in two local pool rooms. I met one of the two so-called friendly but tough guys that I got arrested with at one of the pool rooms. He offered to give me a ride to the Jamaica Avenue shopping area to purchase stage clothes for my group's upcoming tour, but I later learned the men had ulterior motives: They were attracted to my lovely two sisters who wanted to go shopping with me. Although I didn't have an arrest record like those two dudes, I was jailed with them on Rikers Island to await a hearing, even after they told the cops they were only doing a favor for my sisters and me. I'm glad to say my sisters were released without issue after the car chase.

When I was jailed, I knew I had to be ready to stand up for myself and prove I was not to be taken as some kind of punk. I was actually briefed by the two guys I got busted with while on our way to Rikers in a van with other prisoners. Thankfully, when the three of us went to court a few days later, by them admitting to being the actual car thieves and saying I had nothing to do with it, the judge set me free on April 4th — the day before my group went on that 16-day tour.

The tour went very well, which was followed by a week of performances at the Apollo that started on May 2, 1958. The first time I snorted heroin up my nose was while at the Apollo. I recall that day clearly, as it was the day of the Kentucky Derby, and someone brought me a tiny $5.00 bag of that white powder instead of the $5.00 bag of marijuana I told him to get for me. That first sniff ushered in many years of dope use. What also made that week memorable were appearances by the great Black female singer, Ms. Ruth Brown, the comedian Nipsey Russell, the Cha-

Cha Taps, the Kit Kats, Juanita Monroe, and the Cootie Williams backup band.

♫ ♫ ♫ ♫ ♫

While awaiting the release of my trust fund in 1961, I continued to press forward with trying to revitalize the vocal group, all while establishing myself as a drug dealer in Jamaica Queens. Still, music was in my blood, and the need to continue singing was quite powerful. After three recording sessions and eight records as The Teenagers with Billy Lubrano (who had replaced Frankie in October 1957), we did two more cuts in March 1960 with a singer named Kenny Bobo, a close buddy of Frankie Lymon. Then, right after him, we came across a strong Jackie Wilson sound-alike named Freddie Houston and recorded two powerful love songs with him: *Can You Tell Me* and *A Little Wiser Now*, using Sherman in an extraordinary bass opening line. Artie Ripp, a young Italian man, aided us in getting a recording with a company known as End Records after I happened to show him and his group how to truly sing as a group of five.

In January 1961, Freddie Houston was no longer with The Teenagers. We were a four-man group with no lead singer. We produced a song titled *What's on*

Your Mind as "Joey and The Teenagers," and then as "Sherman and The Teenagers," singing a western-style song called *The Draw*. Eventually, we picked up a female lead singer introduced to us by Nick Quesado of The Colts. The Colts were first managed by Buck Ram, who also managed The Platters, and he produced a hit song for them called *Adorable*. (Both of those great vocal groups were with us during our very first April-June 1956 tour.) After Nick became interested in managing us, which happened to be the day that we ran into him while he was auditioning a female singer, Sandra Dawn, it was at that time at Harlequin rehearsal studio in New York City that we agreed. He quickly got us a Columbia Records deal where we recorded *I Hear the Angels Sing*, *Wild Female*, and three others. Sandra was an awesome-looking lady who got us attention.

Importantly, Nick was also very instrumental in making sure we were free to use "The Teenagers" as our group name. That was a necessary step due to Roulette Records' owner, Morris Levy, having complete control and ownership of what was turned over to him by George Goldner which included our royalties. A man by the name of Joe Kolski was assigned to get us to put our signatures on a one-page document giving Goldner all our group name rights, but we wisely refused to sign. I still find it hard to believe they wanted to move us out of the picture altogether. I suppose they operated out of fear of us getting in the way of their efforts to enlarge Frankie Lymon as a solo artist while basically destroying our whole group's 'Rage of the Age' global fame.

Moving on...

Sandra Dawn was not only a phenomenal Frankie Lymon replacement, but she was also a 'super pinch-hitter' (as they say in baseball). In fact, when my first wife and I briefly moved to an apartment in Brooklyn in April 1961, and I shared the address with Sandra Dawn, she told me that she had gone out with a gentleman who lived next door to us who was very jealous of her. After first meeting her mom and then meeting her, Nick thought to add her to our group, which came to be immediately in 1961 for six months. Sandra Dawn worked with us in theatres known as the "Chitlin Circuit": the Howard Theater in Washington, DC; the Uptown Theatre in Philadelphia, PA; the Royal Theater in Baltimore, MD; the Fox Theater in Detroit, MI; and, of course, the Apollo Theatre in Harlem, NY. Sandra left our group in September, replacing Zola Taylor of The Platters.

♫ ♫ ♫ ♫ ♫

I suggest putting on your seat belt for what I'm about to share next. (You can remove it after the next paragraph.)

Now, regarding my group's so-called trust funds that were held until we turned 21 in 1961, it is important to note that the amounts dispersed were the end of any financial obligations toward our singers' royalties from 1956 to 1961. Throughout those years, there were all sorts of changes to the group, our monies, and our business dealings. We even hired lawyers and accountants we trusted to watch over our trust funds. When I saw the amount of money being held for me (outside of the little given to my mom all those years), I was floored! On the 18th day of April 1961, the New York court okayed the settlement of our trust funds, which only Joe, Herman, and I were able to receive (Sherman and Frankie had yet to turn 21). The following amounts are exact to the penny, including the funds dispersed to Sherman and Frankie when they came of age: I received **$1,175.99**; Joe Negroni received **$2,783.81**; Herman Santiago received **$2,377.80**; Sherman Garnes received **$1,377.43**; and Frankie Lymon received **$285.27**.

Okay. You can remove your seat belt now. That rough, memorable ride is now over. Five years of hard work, performing and traveling around the globe, landed the five of us meager amounts of money. Even in the 1960s, those amounts were astonishing. Were that same trust fund paid out to me today, it would be valued at **$11,871.44!** Unbelievable, right?! Pennies, dear reader. Pennies! What happened to our money? It was stolen!

Sherman, Joe, Herman, and I had big plans for the money we thought we would receive. Putting our group back together was at the top of the list. Disappointingly, both Nick and Sandra Dawn left us, and those dreams quickly dissipated. By September of that year, we were left with no prospects of performing again.

Earlier that same year, I married my dear, darling girlfriend, Barbara Ann. I was 21; she was 18 and pregnant. We lived together in the Bronx due to us leaving Jamaica Queens after her dad threatened me to leave her be. He didn't like the fact that she spent a lot of time at my mom's away from her parents' home. It must be noted here that I was drug-free for a short time when we got married.

Up to that point in my life, I tried working various types of jobs, including a job at a hamburger spot, mopping floors; making up dorm beds at Creedmoor State Hospital (they found out I lied on my job application about my age and fired me); an aluminum company learning all about machine shop work; and driving for a private taxi company in Brooklyn called Black Pearl Gypsy Cabs.

It's amazing how things concluded in my life in 1961. Sorrowfully, I was being drawn into darkness, adjusting to living in 'the hood.' I used the balance of my trust fund to get into the drug-dealing business — one that quickly failed due to my hired peddler not returning the money he earned so that I could re-up and expand. Despite him being a trusted friend, he was also an addict. (A drug dealer and an addict are never a good combination.) At that time, I was back on dope and became a street person who learned how to hustle in the hood on both sides of town in Jamaica Queens. The pool rooms were where I quickly learned how to make money to support my drug habit.

Amidst it all, I continued to try and maintain my singing career. The very last Teenagers shows were at a club in Staten Island, New York, known as Crocitto's: two on Friday night, November 21st, and two on Saturday night, November 22nd. With Sandra Dawn gone, we used Sherman's girlfriend, Lana Lang Warner, in her place. She did a fabulous job as the lead singer (and later, became the mother of Sherman's first daughter), but that was the end of The Teenagers.

♫ ♫ ♫ ♫ ♫

I recall the time when Sherman and I both needed dope fixes (this happened long before taking Morris Levy to court for our writers' royalties rights in the 1980s). We went to Mr. Levy's office and, upon arrival, were very surprised to see an elite-gifted framed golden record that was awarded to The Teenagers on his large office lobby wall, along with many others that had **nothing** to do with what he did musically for us or them. When we inquired about the award and asked him for some royalty money, he stated, "I own *Why Do Fools Fall in Love* and am entitled to receive all its writers' royalties. George Goldner turned all the rights over to me. Remove yourselves from my office." Sherman and I politely did as he requested.

Interestingly, in January 1956, a very informative, short write-up in Jet Magazine and many others stated that *Why Do Fools Fall in Love* had been written by our 13-year-old lead singer, Frankie Lymon. He was labeled as "a teenager composer," as referenced by Mr. Goldner in his plans to promote Frankie as such. Then, when we met Phil Kahl of Patricia-Kah Music Corp., we learned he, too, was associated with Goldner and Levy and was also involved in the misuse of our record-publishing rights. Phil used to drive us around to interviews in his flashy convertible sports cars in Los Angeles for guest appearances on TV shows. Then, when we returned to New York City, to show us more so-called 'friendliness,' he did the same — all while knowing he did not have our best interests at heart. He, too, was a liar and a thief. Surprisingly, we learned that Morris Levy owned the great jazz club in New York City called "Birdland." It was the same club where Phil Kahl took Frankie and me to see the jazz vocal group that I loved: The Hi-Los.

However, I slowly began learning about our music publishing rights and how their false answers told to us didn't mesh with what I knew. For example, I **knew** our group had broken through the color barrier line. I **knew** we had become a phenomenally successful crossover act with a pint-sized kid named Frankie Lymon. I **knew** we were the first to exit long limousines wearing sneakers and jeans. Those things and countless other moments were proof that my dream became a reality, all while my future still looked dark.

♫ ♫ ♫ ♫ ♫

Now, concerning other informative things about Frankie before again moving forward from the 1950s...

There was a fun moment when Frankie asked me if he could go horseback riding with me in Manhattan's Central Park, which was fine by me. Later, the group and I had a good laugh as I told the story about us being chased by two policemen (also on horseback) due to us galloping our horses as opposed to walking them. Frankie was a belligerent kid at times, even with authoritative people — including how he sassed those two police officers that day. During his one-and-a-half-year period with The Teenagers, I saw that trait in him when he spoke to his mom as well as senior people in show business.

Frankie loved to laugh with us when we played jokes on each other in our connected hotel rooms while on the road under the watchful eye of our road manager. And while Frankie often observed us attracting female teenage fans to our rooms for sex without getting caught, he seemingly looked at us as though he, too, was sexually experienced while copying our every move. He was such a prideful kid.

I sometimes wondered if Frankie told his mom he didn't want to leave our group, even though he (and everyone else) knew he was an outstanding star performer. Years later, I learned that riding the subway back and forth daily to record his solo records downtown bothered him at times, even as his mother insisted that he go. The fruit of Frankie's labor came from his early 1958 hit song, *Itty Bitty Pretty One* (the record label listed Frankie Lymon and The Teenagers as the artists). Sadly, his mother's desire for him to become more well-known as a solo artist never came to be. Frankie couldn't replicate the hits of the past, primarily due to his voice changing as he got older. As a matter of fact, the same applied to The Teenagers. Our voices changed amid using three replacement lead singers to take Frankie's place. The actual end of The Teenagers came in 1961. Period.

♫ ♫ ♫ ♫ ♫

I believe our original group's downfall resulted from Frankie just being a troubled kid. Joe called my thoughts "nonsense" and said that he was going to "piss on Frankie's grave" after he passed away in 1968 — something that he did with the use of his words in a book that he later wrote. Within, he disregarded the mixed-up kid that Frankie was. For some reason, I found myself feeling my own set of mixed emotions concerning Frankie, especially when I learned about the dirty, unloving heart that he could display.

While married with three children, I immaturely snuck around behind my darling wife's back to get drugs in Harlem from Bobby Phillips of The Cadillacs, who was fresh out of jail (he was the one I trusted with my dope who ripped me off). Something similar happened when I encountered Frankie in 1964 after learning he was performing at the Apollo. I wanted to see him, so I went to the Apollo's backstage entrance. Mr. Spain—a cool Black gentleman who worked there and knew me from my many appearances—let me right in. When Frankie came downstairs, we briefly chatted about our sad breakup before drugs entered the conversation. He promised to buy some for both of us after his last show that evening. When I returned later in need of a fix, after a long wait, Mr. Spain looked at me sadly and said, *"The entire building is empty, Jimmy."* When I asked him about Frankie's whereabouts, he stated, *"Frankie left a long time ago out the front doors."* I was greatly disappointed in how Frankie let me down.

As if to confirm his sad, unfortunate self-thinking, a year later (1965), Frankie sent Joe and Sherman a telegram asking them to record with him. I was with Sherman at the time, heading through his block to purchase and go shoot up our dope, when his mom alerted him about the telegram. We waited until after we got high to read it and were immediately filled with a certain joy. We never suspected that our positive feelings would result in Frankie taking us on yet another negative, disappointing trip once again. In short, although he didn't know my address, he believed I would not have a negative attitude about us backing him up, so he didn't have to send me a direct request. Herman was unavailable at the time. Nonetheless, the three of us got together and agreed to go to the downtown studio to back him up.

Interestingly, Kenny Bobo from Jimmy Castor and The Juniors (whom Frankie knew very well) filled in for Herman for the two songs that Frankie wanted us to sing background on. The session went very well, but after backing up Frankie on those songs and waiting outside the recording studio for the promised $200 a piece, Frankie left us standing. Joe had reached his frustrating end and said, "That's it for me. No more!" Kenny had a pretty good idea of where Frankie had disappeared to—the Gerald Hall rehearsal studio on 119th Street and 7th Avenue—so the three of us went there. Upon our arrival, Kenny violently grabbed Frankie as he tried working his way out the front door. Sherman and I, along with a female friend named Laurita, managed to separate them, and Frankie ran as fast as he could to get away from the beatdown Kenny believed he was due. That was the last time Sherman,

Joe, I saw Frankie alive, but not Kenny and, of course, Herman.

Kenny and Herman lived in the same neighborhood as Frankie and would tell me they saw him hanging out on street corners where drugs could be found, "doing his thing" (just like we all were in the drug world). Three years later, just after I turned 28, we all learned of Frankie Lymon's tragic overdose death that occurred on February 28, 1968. Kenny was the first to learn of it and was so very sorry, as was us all.

CHAPTER 9: THE DARK YEARS – PART 2

Beyond Frankie Lymon's very sad heroin overdose death that occurred in the bathroom of his grandmother's apartment (in the building next to Stitt JHS), I was personally torn to pieces for additional reasons. Along with him being gone from this earth, any prospects of Frankie Lymon and The Teenagers coming together again left with him—something I had hoped for since our separation from him in June 1957, even up until what became the **official** end of The Teenagers group in November 1961. In essence, my personal teenager's dream died with him with great disappointment. At the time, I didn't recognize the true value of my dream that had been placed in my heart by God to be used by and for Him.

Ironically, through the ups and downs of life, I felt as if I was dead. I carried the pains of being separated from my first wife and children while driving a truck making large out-of-town deliveries, along with knowing our original five-boy vocal group would never exist again. It's not too far-fetched to think that it likely would not have happened anyway due to our involvement with the dangers of street life.

It bothers me to be prompted to write in-depth about that time in my life, but God is leading me to do so.

♫ ♫ ♫ ♫ ♫

Despite the thoughts I had of improving my life when my family and I returned to living in Brooklyn, my out-of-hand drug use and street life caused me to be separated from my family. During that time (early 1965 to 1967), I uncaringly continued to purchase and shoot up dope, leading my wife, Barbara, and me to fall behind in bills and her begging me to enter a dope-use detoxification center. Well, I did go. I signed in and then uncaringly signed out the very next day. My love for my life and my wife was not strong enough at the time to be clean.

Before Barbara decided to move away with our three children to another place, I was still working. In fact, I had even come across Sherman, who (coincidently) worked near my job. He and I have always been close since our first meeting in class and were excited about getting back in touch with one another. We would meet after work, drink Thunderbird wine with two of our buddies, buy dope, and shoot up at one of their houses.

Aside from my drug use and constantly trying to fulfill my role as a family man, I also enjoyed playing softball with the employees on my job against other factory softball teams. At times, my six-year-old son, James Jr., would hold on tightly to my back while I played the shortstop position that I loved since I was a child. It was pleasing to know he, too, loved the game. He used to play stickball on the block that his mother relocated to with all our furniture while I was at work one day when she could no longer take any more of my shenanigans. Not long after, I quit working at the factory due to getting sick and moved in with my mother, who lived ten blocks away. While there, I applied for unemployment and left drugs alone. Roughly six weeks later, I got a job driving a truck in Greenpoint Brooklyn, which was the job I had when I learned of Frankie's passing in 1968.

♫ ♫ ♫ ♫ ♫

Speaking of Frankie again... I cannot stress enough just how skilled he was as a 13-year-old performer. As he bounced around in front of the rest of us at our live concerts, his pint-sized self completed "the package," leaving us to look squeaky clean. Teen girls and women alike were attracted to us all (including Frankie). Unfortunately, our teenage and young adult antics led the five of us boys to heartbreak in the so-called show business world. Much like Sherman, Herman, and me, Frankie also became a heavy drug user and soon lost all the great attention he once had as he tried (and failed) to get bookings for club appearances as a solo singer. Primarily due to the negative effects of drug use, he no longer looked nor sounded like the cute kid he once was.

In his late teens and after, Frankie continually battled drug use, was in and out of hospitals, and kept getting busted. An Ebony magazine piece on Frankie stated, *"On June 21, 1966, he [Frankie Lymon] was arrested on a heroin charge and was drafted into the United States Army in lieu of a jail sentence."* He was stationed at Fort Gordon, Georgia, just outside of Augusta. Although he was hardly a model soldier, he was never finicky about staying on the base when he was supposed to be on duty. Eventually, he was released with a less-than-honorable discharge due to drinking bouts and other small offenses.

Life wasn't all bad for Frankie while in Augusta, Georgia. While there, he met and married a respectable elementary school teacher named Emira Eagle. She was instrumental in securing numerous weekend appearances early on in their marriage, all while maintaining her teaching job. Unfortunately, in February 1968, he received a call from his so-called "new manager" in New York City that proved to be the catalyst to his overdose death. In fact, his death certificate reads:

"Acute Intravenous Narcotism"
(Habitual use of narcotics leading to a drug overdose.)

♫ ♫ ♫ ♫ ♫

Not long after Frankie's death, I moved into a three-room, second-floor apartment in Brooklyn, back with my wife and children. The apartment was located on Pacific Street between Howard and Saratoga. My life took a disappointing turn, leading me even further into my own noncaring lifestyle — especially in light of outliving Frankie and experiencing an instance when I passed out from shooting up dope on a Saturday afternoon in the bathroom of a Philadelphia factory where I was making a truck delivery. It might be surprising to you, dear reader, to know my wife was riding with me that day. After patiently awaiting my return, she felt she had waited long enough and proceeded to get out of the truck to look for me. The gentleman on duty who accepted the delivery found me in the bathroom, passed out in a stall after shooting up strong dope and pocketing my drug paraphernalia. To protect me from any potential reprimand, Barbara lied to the man, telling him that I had very little sleep before loading the truck that morning then driving there from Brooklyn. Once I came to and climbed back into the truck, I carefully made my way back to the company I worked for, caught a taxi for us, made it home, and promised her it would never happen again.

I didn't keep my promise.

Due to my inability to stop using drugs, I lost my truck driving job and turned to driving a taxi for the private company mentioned previously. When that didn't work, I drove a private cab for my sister's boyfriend. My efforts to make a sufficient income for my wife and kids were challenging. One weekend, I got into a terrible accident while helping a dope addict buddy. I had given him a ride to a car repair shop and double-parked while he went inside to steal some tools. Due to being seen, he rushed back to the car. As I sped off, we were chased by their mechanic driving a heavy-duty pickup truck. The man quickly caught up to us and blocked the street, cutting me off on Rockaway Boulevard. Cornered, I had to stop abruptly, which caused me to crash into a corner store on the right side of the street. The man got out of his truck with a sledgehammer, yelling for us to exit the car. Instead of doing so, I tried to drive away — but not before he smashed the windshield with the sledgehammer. As I maneuvered my way out of that precarious situation, another car came down the block on my left. It hit my taxi, causing it to roll over to the right upside down. My money-hustling dope buddy crawled out and ran away, as two people aided my exit from the vehicle. They wanted to take me to the hospital, but I asked and insisted that someone just drive me home. Meanwhile, the sledgehammer-wielding guy and I looked at each other and the damage that he caused angrily.

♫ ♫ ♫ ♫ ♫

As those crazy and dangerous events occurred in my life, it took me a while to learn that I had brought them all on myself at age 18 when I first used heroin at the Apollo Theatre. By age 21, I was really strung out. My journey through the darkest years of my life began at that time, ruining my first marriage. Jobs were lost, and I went to jail for six months in October 1969—one-and-a-half years after Frankie's tragic death, which was a very crucial warning for me that I ignored until 1980. In fact, I was caught up in the 'me game,' and it took many years for me to come to grips with the truth.

There was a time when I owned a private taxi that Barbara assisted me in getting. She used some of the insurance money her father left for her when he passed away. In that taxi, an even more serious scenario occurred where I was almost killed...again. That near-death experience changed nothing. I recall it being late Sunday evening, after 11:00 p.m. After what was a busy day of driving the taxi, Barbara called me to pick up her and the children from her grandmother's house in Jamaica, Queens because her uncle had broken his promise to take them home. Of course, I said yes. I then shot some dope, freshened up, and headed out to get them. The primary difference between this instance and the one mentioned previously is that this time, I was taken by ambulance to the hospital—while unconscious. It wasn't until I came to in the emergency room that the doctor was able to tell me what happened...

While driving on a one-way avenue towards Queens, a car coming across on my right side went through the stop sign and crashed into my car. I was sent sailing into a corner building and knocked unconscious, nearly smashing me to death inside my vehicle. When I asked about the other driver, the doctor stated that after his car crashed into mine, it went up the street a few yards and crashed into a parked car. The driver was ejected, hit his head on a fire extinguisher, and was killed. Although I was stunned about not having any physical damage whatsoever, I was very bothered by the death of the other man.

The following morning, two detectives came to my house with an arrest warrant. They shared with me that a bottle of alcohol was in the seat next to the other driver but that I was the one being charged with Vehicular Homicide. What they didn't tell me was that they were aware I was a drug addict and that it was likely I was high or possibly nodding at the wheel, incapable of stopping in time or even beeping my horn to save the life of the other driver before he drove through the stop sign. The charge against me was dropped after the investigation showed the other driver was at fault, which was great work by my legal aid attorney. To this day, I still shoulder guilt. Even though my life was spared, were it not for my drug use before getting behind the wheel that night, his life might have been spared, too. Conversely, had I made it safely to my wife and children that night, only God knows what could have happened to us on our way home.

As I write these words about my life and important music history, other disturbing instances come to mind.

One evening, I was almost stabbed to death in front of Barbara by two men in our second-floor apartment's kitchen as my three children slept in the open-door bedroom next to it. Once again, it was all about drugs and my misuse of the money that was supposed to be returned to one of the men. At one point, I considered trying to get away by jumping out of the front window, but I was saved by my wife, begging them not to kill me as I struggled with them on the kitchen floor. I recall her grabbing the wrist of the one with the knife, begging him not to kill me and that I would get his money to him.

Another time, a large-scale drug czar with a scary reputation sent a carload of four men to look for me after I kept ducking him for not paying his money after I sold his drugs. Once again, my life was spared. I took my family to my sister's house to hide away until things calmed down and we were safe to return home.

Do you see how God kept saving me from what I was not born to do?

♫ ♫ ♫ ♫ ♫

Those very unpleasant experiences and death-defying incidents that I lived through are discomforting to reveal. I often pause to stop and think, *"How can I pen my truths in a way that will not discourage the reader from wanting to continue reading?"* Prayer is a powerful tool, my friend. While this is my life, this is **GOD'S** story that must be told so that He will get the glory. Just when I thought I should soften the words, the Spirit provided correction and assured me my story will be received in the spirit it is shared. As such, I choose to move forward with more tales concerning 'The Dark Years' of my life with the hope and prayer that you will be blessed in the end.

At one point, I wrestled with a family issue that popped up with my son, causing me to be more stuck in this writing process than ever before. I shut down my writing and went to bed. The following morning, I talked with God while having my morning coffee and was led to insert the essential spiritual information for my reader (you) to learn more about focusing on God in our lives through thick and thin. Additionally, it's imperative that, during these difficult times globally, we see things from a Godly, spiritual perspective.

As stated, I was led by the Holy Spirit to move forward with sharing with you—from a spiritual/biblical viewpoint—how to deal with challenges in our lives. It would be wise of us to come to grips with how God sees things through our ups and downs in life and learn the lessons He teaches us, including being used by Him when we least expect it.

For example, although I didn't know it at the time, all those death-threatening experiences I endured are now being used by God to demonstrate that He was and is **always** there for His purposes. My friend, God is our Lifesaver! His Son, Jesus Christ, teaches us all how to see every single thing from a Godly perspective. Being in touch with Him both prayerfully and biblically is critical to our spiritual health to be used of Him. There is no other way, my friend. None.

The best biblical example is the temptation of Jesus while in the wilderness **(Luke 4:1-13, NIV):**

"Jesus, full of the Holy Spirit, left the Jordan and was led by the Spirit into the wilderness, where for forty days, He was tempted by the devil. He ate nothing during those days, and at the end of them, He was hungry. The devil said to Him, 'If you are the Son of God, tell this stone to become bread.' Jesus answered, 'It is written: 'Man shall not live on bread alone.'' The devil led Him up to a high place and showed Him in an instant all the kingdoms of the world. And he said to Him, 'I will give you all their authority and splendor; it has been given to me, and I can give it to anyone I want to. If You worship me, it will all be Yours.' Jesus

answered, 'It is written: 'Worship the Lord your God and serve Him only.'' The devil led Him to Jerusalem and had Him stand on the highest point of the temple. 'If You are the Son of God, throw Yourself down from here. For it is written: 'He will command His angels concerning You to guard You carefully; they will lift You up in their hands, so that You will not strike Your foot against a stone.'' Jesus answered, 'It is said: 'Do not put the Lord your God to the test.'' When the devil had finished all this tempting, he left Him until an opportune time.''

After that last verse, Jesus went to Nazareth (where He was raised as a child) and was rejected by the people there. He then returned to Galilee in the power of the Holy Spirit, where He taught in their synagogues, and everyone praised Him.

You see, Jesus came to earth as a human to show us how to deal with life from a spiritual standpoint. He dealt with the devil while in the wilderness by denying what the devil believed were Christ's "fleshly needs." In Jesus' humanness, we know the wilderness temptation challenge was His last. He is the same One who was nailed to a wooden cross to die for our sins, but not before going through a temptation far beyond anything we will ever experience. We must remain steadfast and unmovable through to the rapture — the moment when God brings His Godly people in Christ to Heaven. But know this: The devil will never give up on gaining souls for Hell. He is always looking for an opportunity to "do us in," which is why we must study the Word of God and know it for ourselves (read 2 Timothy 2:15). It is what being a true Christian is all about!

1 Peter 4:12-13 (NIV) makes what we will endure plain and clear:

"Dear friends, do not be surprised at the painful trial you are suffering, as though something strange were happening to you. But rejoice that you participate in the sufferings of Christ, so that you may be overjoyed when His glory is revealed."

Overall, what we must learn in this life is that we cannot please everyone. We are designed to be who God made us to be in both character and personality. He fights our battles and will not allow us to be continually disrespected. We are basically wasting His time when we try to win over people or attempt to change their disapproval of us. My personal lesson here is coming to the realization that "the joy of the Lord is **my** strength" (read Nehemiah 8:10).

♫ ♫ ♫ ♫ ♫

I find it challenging to express all the insurmountable amounts of negativity that I experienced throughout my life, especially when taking into account those spiritual truths that were yet to be made known to me when I was "down and out." My downfall—my slimy past—started with sniffing heroin out of a small, stamp-size cellophane bag to get high and led to shooting that dope into my arms' veins. The process is ugly and dirty, involving the use of hypodermic needles, spoons, water, and a cooker. On the street, heroin had many names: "Junk," "Stuff," "Doogie," and countless others, all dependent upon to whom you were speaking. I, my friend, was a dope addict who shot up that stuff for 22 years.

After living through those death-defying street-life years, I wisely chose to seek out a cure for my addiction. The cure was found at Manhattan's Morris Bernstein Hospital. There, a medication known as Methadone was (and still is) being used medically to replace dope use. Methadone aids addicted men and women to carry on with their lives as they go through a detoxification process of being free from drugs. By October 1, 1980, I was finally free from being a junkie—but was I really?

Mentally, I wasn't quite "there." In fact, thinking I could go right back to work while still healing, I returned to driving my private cab again. I just knew I could trust myself. Well...

The first thing I did after my first paying customer was drove to purchase a bag of dope! I then quickly parked my car in front of a Harlem "shoot-up" location, rushed upstairs, paid $5.00 to shoot up...and overdosed. My life "left me" that day. I woke up in a hospital emergency room, where my life was returned. God once again saved me from my fourth and final dope overdose.

To this day, I never learned whom God used to rush me to the hospital or even how my taxi was safely returned to its garage. As I write these words, all I can say is, **"WOW!"**

♫ ♫ ♫ ♫ ♫

So, my friend, as you will see in my second book (that chronicles my life from 1980 to present-day), dope use and life-threatening issues came to an end in this book—but the devil wasn't through with his attacks.

This is not a bunch of nonsense; it's seriously all about life. Just as the devil was not done with Jesus after being outwitted by Jesus in the wilderness, he is always out to get both you and me. The devil even tried working through a woman I was in a relationship with. Yes, he tried to do me in while I was working on trying to get my life together after ruining my first marriage. That relationship led me to allow God to step into my life. My friend, God wants to be first and foremost in our lives, just like he was with Jesus Christ, who went through Hell for all humankind on God's behalf. He wants us to be led and guided by Him in this falling-apart world. We must come to grips with God being #1 in our lives. No kidding! He is the only way to go.

In the Bible, Jesus was questioned by His disciples, asking about who could be saved. Jesus replied, *"With men, this is impossible, but with God, all things are possible"* (read Matthew 19:26).

As humans, we tend to have a questioning mentality that can keep us stuck "in the wilderness. We often focus on our past instead of constantly looking forward, trusting in the promises of God and His Word. Daily, I'm reminded to move forward from that mindset of the past.

Briefly, another excellent Bible example is Job. At the beginning of his life, all was very well. Then, everything in his life fell apart. Through 37 chapters of the Bible, he lost all that he had. The end of his story came when he listened to the wisdom of God. His spiritual eyes were opened, and everything he lost was restored. Such it was with my life. Three things made a difference and provided restoration: Giving God my time, going to church, and reading the Bible.

Know this: Your 'waiting time' doesn't mean being passive. It means actively "walking by faith, and not by sight" (read 2 Corinthians 5:7). The day will come when you will see God for **His** wisdom and understanding—*not your own.*

CHAPTER 10: THE DARK YEARS – PART 3

Returning now to the 1950s…

I want to share with you a few words about my first darling wife, Barbara Ann, as well as details concerning the 'A-side' of Frankie Lymon and The Teenagers' fifth hit song, *I'm Not a Juvenile Delinquent*, recorded in late 1956.

I'm Not a Juvenile Delinquent was (notably) the first "protest" song. The words object to being labeled as 'bad,' but eclipse with a strong, uplifting truth in its opening line. While looking at me, Barbara would smile and lovingly sing the words, right along with Frankie:

"Do the thing that's right, and you'll do nothing wrong, and life will be so nice, and you'll be in paradise. I know… because I'm not a juvenile delinquent."

During that same time, *Baby Baby, Teenage Love*, and *Paper Castles* were recorded.

I met Barbara before her 13th birthday at the end of 1956. Our family lived three blocks from where Barbara and her family lived in Jamaica, Queens. She, like many females, was far more mentally mature than other boys her age or even older (something I quickly learned about Barbara in comparison to girls I was with before her after speaking with her at length).

Other times, she would quote the following words to me (also from *I'm Not a Juvenile Delinquent*) with sweet humility:

"It's easy to be good; it's hard to be bad. Stay out of trouble, and you'll be glad. Now, take this tip from me, and you will see how happy you will be."

If only I could say I had acted on those words. If I did, I would feel better about writing about my life story today...

Moreover, as far as Barbara is concerned, that was a relationship in which I failed — miserably. I was blinded by the devil from that point in time until the age of 45 when God stepped into my life. I'm truly grateful that He did **when** He did — as we all should be. It is all about His timing, not ours! Amen?

Moving along.

I'm Not a Juvenile Delinquent came to our group through me (initially) from an older songwriter friend, Robert Spencer, whom I knew from a chance meeting at the Apollo. That evening, Spencer (as I called him) filled in as a singer for The Cadillacs. Aware of my musical skills, when we ran into each other and talked, due to his persistence about my group recording a song he penned, I called George Goldner and arranged for them to meet. The meeting took place days later, just before my group had an interview at the downtown NYC Brill Building — the "Epicenter of Pop Music" at the time. In fact, loads of R&B leading songwriters did business there, oftentimes even in front of the building, trying to get people interested in their songs. (It was also the location where our 'Cash Box' magazine interview took place.) After Spencer shared his song with us, we fell in love with it instantly. In particular, Frankie and Sherman loved the words. When George's limo pulled up, he jumped out, introduced himself to Spencer, and then led us into the building. On the ride up to George's office in the elevator, Spencer again sang his song, Juvenile Delinquent, to us. Immediately, we all began grooving to the beat, right along with Spencer. Seeing that all five of us boys were into it, George saw the possibility of another hit song and invited Spencer to his office while we boys made our way to our interview location. Later, Spencer shared the following with us:

"Being that writers' royalties take time to receive, Mr. Goldner offered me cash to buy I'm Not a Juvenile Delinquent, which I accepted."

Such was the crazy music business at the time, **especially** with George Goldner.

♬ ♬ ♬ ♬ ♬

Back to Barbara...

She was a fascinating yet quiet little ladylike girl with a classy body, beautifully shaped legs, and a maturity level beyond her years. She was stared at wherever she went and was admired by her family and my sister Jean, who introduced us when I got home from doing shows at the end of 1956. While desiring and earning her own money, Barbara received money from her father, Bobby Lakins. He was a former boxer who drove around the city as a number-betting collector, picking up money and numbers from people who played (he also paid those who hit their numbers). Barbara was also adored by four uncles who gave her money if and when needed. On the weekends, she worked at a beauty salon, preparing ladies for their hairdos. On the rare occasion when she played hooky from school, I politely corrected her decision, further demonstrating my care for her.

Barbara regularly came over to visit my sister Jean. There were also times Barbara would visit our home and spend the night with me in my bedroom. One day, I (being my usual bold, flirty self) was taking a bath and asked Jean, *"Can you please ask Barbara to come in and wash my back?"* I'm sure you can imagine how floored she and Barbara were by my boldness, even though I explained I would respectfully "cover myself" with a towel. At the time, I had countless girls sending me letters from all over the country. I came to know and like some of them, but something about Barbara made her extra special. Jean and Barbara giggled and laughed, as schoolgirls do, but in the end, Barbara fulfilled my not-so-innocent request. From that day on, that beautiful young girl and I were involved—even as she sometimes observed me entertaining a redheaded Jewish girl named Sherry (whom I had an enormous crush on).

Not to excuse myself from being a female chaser, I later explained to Barbara that being a singer in a vocal group was a fad that drew attention and attracted girls. Unlike street rollerskating, singing was a 'quality fad' that was directly tied to getting girls— an aspect of being a vocal artist that continues to this day for both male and female singers. Barbara then shared with me that she witnessed relationship struggles with the men in her family, including the difficulties her parents (who were separated) experienced. However, despite constantly being drawn to having a closeness with various girls, while it did some harm later in my life, it did not interfere with my marriage to Barbara.

While chasing girls and women was not uncommon for us men, there were other things that proved more detrimental to our lives. For me, that list included overdoing it with booze, popping pills, smoking marijuana, and getting hooked on drugs. All those things eventually did irreparable damage to my life as a married man with children. Early on, the other Teenagers (including Frankie) and I were greatly influenced by the older male performers as we watched and imitated how they drew females to them, both on and off the stage. Some of those influencers included Frank Sinatra, Billy Eckstine, Nat King Cole, Johnny Mathis, Elvis Presley, Jackie Wilson, Tony Williams of The Platters, and Little Anthony of The Imperials. I can't forget to mention Teddy Randazzo who sang relationship songs including *I'm On the Outside Looking In* and *Hurt So Bad*.

It didn't take long for Barbara and me to fall in love. What began as young people with a crush on each other grew to be true love, starting when my group returned to Hollywood, California, to perform on Walter Winchell's "Shower of Stars" TV show on Friday, December 21, 1956. Before leaving for that performance, I told Barbara I would wave at her as I looked directly into the camera. When I got back home, she said she waved back at the TV when she saw me wave at her.

Barbara Ann and I got married on February 12, 1961, after she turned 18 years old. At the time, she was pregnant. While going through the thick and thins of life, she gave me five beautiful children: James Jr. Yancy (June 1961); Jamise Ann (July 1962); Scott Brady (September 1964); Solideen (February 1973); and Star (January 1980). Star was critical in helping me put an end to my 'Dark Years.'

♫ ♫ ♫ ♫ ♫

Going briefly back down memory lane to my time on Rikers Island, where I got the desire to write my life story in December 1969, after seeing the Jackson 5 on TV...

My desire to sing on oldies shows was revived. I also realized just how gifted I was as an artist, doing remarkable pencil drawings that kept me busy after Sherman, Herman, and James Stanley left. I couldn't wait to get out! While in Rikers, I recognized that, aside from music, I could have mastered art and gone into business. Some of the artwork I completed while in Rikers included pencil portraits of my mom, oldest son, myself, well-known personalities, a Black nude woman stretch dancing, and another of a lady with an almost see-through slip-over to her upper thighs. (I shaded her completely with an afro, with my wife, Barbara, in mind.)

When I was released from Rikers in March 1970, I rented a room on Bergen Street, two blocks from where we lived on Pacific Street. In order to collect welfare money, I told the agency that I was separated from my wife. Sadly, I immediately resorted to doing drugs again. In 1971, the Methadone Maintenance Treatment Program in New York City accepted me and placed me on 30 milligrams daily to help beat the habit. In 1973, a better treatment facility in Brooklyn known as the Addiction Research & Treatment Corporation (A.R.T.C.) contacted me, so I made the change. (I have a buddy named Etienne Mauge' who had a relative who worked there as a director. My son, Solideen, also happens to be employed at that location at 937 Fulton Street, but they have since changed their name.) When I got accepted, there were a few others I knew in show business also on the methadone treatment program like me. In June 1971, I was featured in their spotlight column, 2nd 'Spokesman Publication', about both my music career and artistic abilities. In October 1971, my artwork was on exhibition at their location — all attempts to provide stability in my life. It was all to no avail.

♫ ♫ ♫ ♫ ♫

Amazingly, after doing nothing for 11 years, The Teenagers got back together again from February to June 1973, with a fantastic female lead singer: Pearl McKinnon. It was a great moment in time in terms of our reunion. I was once again overjoyed about the prospect of reviving the fame we once had. I could feel it in the air! Unfortunately, I had no idea it would all come crashing down four months later. I fondly recall the very last time our original group was on stage with a unique female Frankie Lymon sound-alike. The experience was phenomenally breathtaking! Pearl was a professional singing beauty. Her addition to the group came about when the well-known vocal group producer, Larry Marshack, first contacted me, asking if I might be interested in bringing the group back together for shows. One, in particular, was "The

Geator with the Heater," with Jerry Blavat. Jerry was a Rock 'n Roll radio deejay who did stage shows as well. Larry had another buddy, "Big Bob," whom he told me to call to get in touch with Pearl. Both men knew she could mimic Frankie's style with us very well, and did so phenomenally.

After practicing and preparing her for performances, we sang in a few small venues which led to us doing three big engagements. The first was two big shows at the Civic Center in Philadelphia, PA on March 17, 1973, for Jerry Blavat with the following huge stars: Johnny Maestro and The Crests, Benny King, Fabian, Ronnie Spector and The Ronettes, The Skyliners, Dion, and Little Richard. Then, after performing at a few other small venues, we did another Philadelphia show at the Academy of Music in May 1973 for only $800 (I believe that was the same payment as the first performance). The third big show was at the New York Academy of Music (the very last show with the four of us original Teenagers). In fact, we performed twice on Saturday, June 16th, 1973: one show at 8:00 p.m., and the other at 11:00 p.m. The concert was presented by Rock Magazine, titled "The 14th Original Rock & Roll Show." Other vocal groups on the list included The Marvelettes, Fleetwoods, Kingston Trio, Duprees, Channels, Richard Barrett and The Valentines, Moonglows, Nutmegs, and The

Pastels. John Zacherle, an American television host and radio personality, was the emcee of that event.

As I write about my experience all these years later, I realize that another shot at our group's fame—another shot at my lifelong dream being fulfilled—left us again when Pearl McKinnon departed after those four amazing months. No Frankie Lymon. No Pearl McKinnon. I was **done**.

Eddy Rezzonico—a very responsible all-around younger group singer whom Herman and I still know today—tried to encourage us to still work on re-forming the group in the summer of 1974. He was signing in Las Vegas at the time when he called me, asking if I was interested in coming there to also sing. To this day, Eddy and I still laugh about my immediate response to his question that came in the form of a question: *"Do they have any methadone programs there?"* (Drug use was still a major issue in my life at the time, all the way up until 1980.)

Barbara wanted our family to do better, so she agreed to relocate to an apartment in the Bronx that Herman's girlfriend, Rita (whom he later married), caringly told us about. Rita believed Herman and I still had a chance to make things happen by living near each other. Honestly, I wanted nothing more to do with the vocal group stuff, to the point that it took a lot of convincing for me to even accept an interview that year from the Associate Editor of a leading oldies vocal group magazine called 'Bim Bam Boom.' The interview was with the late Phil Groia, a Stitt JHS teacher who later became my friend and wrote a book titled *They All Sang on the Corner*, stemming from the story of The Harptones — a Doo-Wop group formed in 1953 that never had a Top 40 pop hit (I knew their lead singer, Willie Winfield, and their pianist/arranger, Raoul Cita). My first daughter's mother, Vickie Burgess, also worked with them.

♫ ♫ ♫ ♫ ♫

Music sort of popped back into my life, although somewhat differently, during that 1974 period back in the Bronx. While still on methadone, I made a living for my family by working for an Italian gentleman named Nick. He owned frankfurter wagons on Amsterdam Avenue and 168th Street and then began selling pennants that he personally made for baseball and football games. Then, he began following music performers such as Marvin Gaye, Stevie Wonder, The Jacksons, The Osmond Brothers, and others, selling t-shirts, photos, and pennants with their photos on them. I was one of Nick's best hustlers, good at working our way into selling those items in parking lots and getting inside arenas and theatres. We even worked our way off the street into nearby entrances and ramps of places like Yankee Stadium, Ebbets Field (where the Brooklyn Dodgers played), and the Polo Grounds in Upper Harlem (where the NY Giants played). On one occasion, Nick got the management to allow us to work inside during Elvis Presley's intermission due to our interference selling outside. While working on an upper balcony section slightly above the stage, when Elvis came out, waving and walking around the stage, he saw me and stopped — likely wondering who the Black man was selling pennants during his intermission, especially because most of his followers were White. I, of course, was stunned to see him that close-up.

When I would return home after selling merchandise souvenirs with Nick's team of five guys, my marriage continued to suffer. My drug issues persisted, leading to my lack of true responsibility for my marriage to Barbara and the fatherhood of our four children. More and more, she began to separate herself from me. I knew I loved Barbara and my children deeply, yet that drug beast rode my back relentlessly. I have many fond memories of our time together, including our daughter's first day of school and her June 1976 JHS graduation when I took many family pictures.

I had no problem working closer to home independently. I used to sell men's hats, baseball caps, women's jewelry, and pocketbooks in Downtown Manhattan as a licensed street peddler. I also worked parades with Solideen and at Madison Square Garden in 1979, with my oldest son, Yancy, and my nephew, Abraham, working for me. While battling drug use, I never gave up on trying my best to show love to all of them, especially my two oldest sons, Scott and Yancy. I remember going back and forth to their schools, looking to keep them in line as they became harder and harder to handle, getting into trouble that sadly led both to the street-life...just like me.

In 1976, I met with a St. Albans, Queens vocal group that a lady friend of my father wanted to happen through the singer, Al Green. Although the four boys were excellent singers, it never came to be. Another brief vocal group experience came when a group called "The Ebony Stars" had a manager who advertised tryouts for them. It was a group I heard previously in Jamaica, Queens at the Harlequin Rehearsal Studios on 46th Street in downtown New York City. They sang like "Earth, Wind, and Fire," but after one show, I saw no future and departed. Then, my Teenagers buddy, Sherman Garnes, came into the picture, starting with a phenomenal headshot photo of him that I removed from the Harlequin billboard (I still have that photo today). Importantly, the image included an advertisement about a tribute on his behalf scheduled for October 24, 1976, while he was still recuperating from a heart operation. The event was sponsored by Ken "Spiderman" Webb, a WBLS deejay, and the performer/producer/promoter, Chris Curry, who wanted to manage me in 1978. Hundreds attended the affair, along with Joe, Herman, and me. Others in attendance included Lewis Lymon, Three Degrees, J.R. Bailey, Ronnie Dyson, The Cleftones, and Bobby J (a deejay). It was great seeing Sherman, although it was evident he was in a bad state of mind and wasn't taking care of himself. Despite myself and others advising him to do so, he sorrowfully passed away on March 26, 1977.

Both Sherman's and Elvis' deaths—both from drug circumstances, and both in 1977—left me feeling dead, too. Continued drug use wreaked havoc in my life and eventually aided in tearing me apart from my wife and children. That's what drug use does. Even while in a methadone program in the Bronx, trying to "help myself," I was caught in a nearby Spanish Cuchifrito's Restaurant by a staff member, selling my methadone medication to purchase dope so that I could shoot up. I got kicked off that program.

Meanwhile, Barbara did her best to raise our four children while uncomfortably living with her mother in Jamaica, Queens. When our son, Scott, was 13, a lack of discipline and difficulties at school became serious issues. I, of course, followed up with the teacher and received a thank you note in response for being a "rare, caring parent" (I felt I didn't deserve those kind words, even though I did the best I could to discipline my son). In 1977, I found a nicer Bronx apartment for $225.00 a month. That relocation changed nothing. Even after struggling to get on welfare for my family, my hard work amounted to nothing. My personal recklessness as a father was very visible to my children, and Vickie (the mother of my oldest daughter, Victoria) wisely kept her distance from me.

Speaking of daughters: While Barbara was separated from our four kids and me in 1979, she came to visit us one weekend in April and got pregnant with our daughter Star—something I did not know until months later after running into Barbara in Harlem. I had to care for our kids due to her having a hard time with them, but before that moment in time, I briefly dealt with two separate women who were "Teenagers" fans. I met them at the Tropicana Bar and Grill located on Broadway and 169th Street, where Herman and I would meet up for beers, and I would sell them ladies' hats and popular mood rings. I was still trying to survive as a friendly, independent street hustler, all while experiencing discomfort concerning my marriage deep inside.

Unknowingly, I was spiritually confused. The Holy Bible clearly states what the true total need is in our lives:

"Thomas said to Him, 'Lord, we don't know where You are going, so how can we know the way?' Jesus answered, 'I am the way and the truth and the life. No one comes to the Father, except through Me'" (John 14:5-6, NIV).

Jesus gave us an across-the-board answer. In other words, there is no true success in life without God, particularly in these very difficult times. With His love for all humankind, God continues to operate behind the scenes of each of our lives, wanting us to make it to Heaven, not Hell. It is imperative that we come to grips with the truth and accept His Son, Jesus Christ, as our personal Lord and Savior who laid down His life for us. Like Jesus, we are to be used by God to witness and lead others to Him. In fact, I'm being led to share how God worked His way into my life that began as a musical dream from Him.

♫ ♫ ♫ ♫ ♫

The Tropicana Bar location referenced earlier was the same location I observed from my Bronx window beginning at age five. Significantly, while it was where my group and our hit song, *Why Do Fools Fall in Love*, came to be, it's just as important to note that it was where God brought Clementine Campbell into my life 45 years later—a Christian woman who led me to Christ on Thanksgiving Day in 1985. It was God's protective hand that kept me from being done in by a bitter woman who worked at the bar. That woman had a deep, inner pain that stemmed from a man who scarred her face with a straight razor. (Let's just add that experience to the list of drug overdoses, thugs, and near-death auto accidents that I was saved from by God.)

I first met Clementine in 1978 at a different bar, two blocks down Broadway, across from Presbyterian Hospital on 168th Street where she worked. From 1978 to 1980, when I entered another A.R.T.C. Methadone Program near where she lived called "The Third Horizon," located at 2195 Third Avenue, our friendship grew. Things began with Clementine and me, starting with her love for the nice ladies' hats I sold. During our two-year span, she spent time in the bar with a lady friend whose boyfriend was a buddy of mine from the Bronx. This, of course, was before Clementine became a Christian woman knowing Jesus as her personal Lord and Savior—details I will dive deeply into in my second book (during 1985).

Another story I am led to share concerns God's protection. One night, while riding the subway train to visit Clementine, I fell asleep after making money selling hats that day. Some street dude on the train cut my back pants pocket with a straight razor, removed my wallet, and stole all the money out of it. He then left my wallet on the seat next to me. Another gentleman woke me up after seeing the wallet and alerted me to the theft. Just think: Had I awoken as that thievery occurred, my life might have been taken, but it was saved by God again. From that day forward, I was more careful and cut down on drinking cheap Thunderbird wine.

While on the A.R.T.C. program near Clementine's apartment, I was deeply involved with the "Third Horizon" art exhibit and singing with a group of guys I put together. Once again, I felt musically inclined. The magnificent coordinator, Ms. Hilda Simms, was a former Black actress who did a film with Sidney Poitier and was the first Black woman on the cover of Ebony magazine. Ms. Simms knew my abilities, both musically and artistically. I shared with Joe Negroni some things about her, due to his association with Hollywood. In fact, Joe was Darby Lloyd Rains' manager — a woman he made into an actress after first making her a singer. She was whose lap he laid his head on when his body was racked with pain before dying from a stroke on September 5, 1978. Before his death, he humbly encouraged and reminded me that along with artistic gifts, I was very capable of returning to the stage. He also advised that I remain independent of Herman due to our significant differences concerning the direction of our group and that I should follow up with Ms. Simms, which I did. Ms. Simms presented my artwork and me to the New York Library Astor, Lenox Ft. Tilden Foundation Art Show at the New York Public Library with other known artistic individuals for a full month, from early October to November. A few of my 13 works on display were the dancer-actor, Bill "Bojangles" Robinson; singer-actor Harry Belafonte; music composer Beethoven; comedian Redd Foxx; and professional boxer Muhammad Ali.

The time in my life came when I no longer wanted to be attached to methadone or any other kind of drug. An experience concerning my historic Doo-Wop dream busted out and began working its way back into my thoughts and life while trying to care for my four children as a single father. I was first contacted by someone who knew the CBS-FM Rock 'n Roll Disc Jockey, Don K. Reed, who then set up an interview for me on October 16, 1978. Don, whom I came to truly respect, also questioned the three group singers with me whom I had auditioned while thinking about re-forming a Teenagers group. Their names were John Langford (from A.R.T.C.), Philip Vere (whom I grew up with in the Bronx), and Ray Wilson (a respectful, awesome vocalist I knew). Coincidently, beside us that day was another guest on Don's show named Richard Nader who did shows when I was on Rikers Island. (Richard stated to me that he wanted to use my Teenagers group if ever I put one back together.)

I am truly appreciative of Ms. Hilda Simms' efforts and encouragement as she began setting up my methadone detoxification program from 90 milligrams daily to zero. I then began looking for a smaller apartment for just myself, my daughter Jamise, and my youngest son Solideen. Sadly, my other great sons, Yancy and Scott, were too deep into street life at the time—something I hurt about.

Wanting my wife back, I needed to be drug-free once and for all. I believe Barbara might have kept her pregnancy with our last child, Star, hidden from me had I not accidentally run into her in Harlem and then realized she got pregnant the last time she visited me.

"This child is yours," she said.

"I'm here for you," I replied with the utmost sincerity and respect. In fact, I am more thankful today than ever before. Star is a loving daughter.

When Star was born on January 16, 1980, because I was not yet drug-free when Barbara asked me to take her, we both agreed to put her up for adoption. I'm **blessed** to say the Lord gave her back to me on August 8, 2011 — 31 years and seven months after her birth.

Clementine, whom I was still seeing and staying with after giving up my Bronx apartment, aided me in finding placement for Jamise and Solideen in temporary foster care until I was able to properly care for them. (I'm smiling right now as I think of him walking with me to and from A.R.T.C. at noon, wanting hot dogs as we passed food trucks on the street. I'm pleased to say we're still close today, just as he is with his own son, Bryan. My daughter before him, Jamise, is a very darling child, taking after her mother.) In February 1980, my caring sister, Alice, gave me her Sunnyside, Queens apartment. (I maintained that small, one-bedroom apartment just off Queens Blvd. at 45-54 39th Place, for 16 years.)

I grew tired of waking up too broke to pay my rent while coming off methadone, so I got a job with a company called "Danite," driving a private taxi that I planned to buy from them. In late September, when it was nearly time for me to switch to an inpatient stay at Morris Bernstein Hospital in Manhattan to complete my detox, out of the clear blue, my two oldest sons approached me, needing somewhere to live. Despite my love and care for them, I should not have agreed to the arrangement, primarily because their hood street life was detrimental to my mental health. For the week that followed their sudden reappearance, I was torn between allowing them to stay in my home while I was to be away, primarily following through with my detoxification set up for me in the hospital for a few weeks.

As I sit here and recall that unsettling point in time, all I can say is **God stepped in!**

One night, while driving my private taxi, and not knowing what to do about my "situation," I picked up a friendly gentleman who happened to be an organ player on his way to a church on 116th Street in Harlem. He stated it was a prayer service night and invited me in, especially after finding out who I was. With empathy, he stated the Deacon there, who once had drug issues like me, would be willing to pray for me. I shed a tear. When he saw how out of it I was, he said, *"Please park in front of the church."* Once inside, I was prayed over upstairs by a bunch of Black women who wore all white and no makeup. My thoughts immediately flashed back to my grandmother's house when I was seven years old, observing the women in a circle who prayed for various things — including the salvation of their children's children. After the prayer session, we went downstairs. That's when an incredible experience took place. The Deacon whom the musician in the taxi referenced was delighted to meet me.

"I got high with Frankie Lymon once," he said.

Testing him, I asked, "Where?"

"At Gerald Halls Studios on 119th Street," he replied without hesitation.

That, of course, amazed me. It also reminded me of the very last time I saw Frankie alive, which, in fact, was there. That Deacon was a changed man who then prayed a powerful prayer over me and my entire family after instructing me to confess Jesus as my personal Lord and Savior—which I did. Immediately afterward, an inspired young sister-in-Christ rushed over to me as I departed and gave me her August 1980 copy of "Our Daily Bread" booklet. She added a Godly farewell kiss on my cheek. I noticed she had penned a few Godly words on it and signed her name: Sis. Angelina.

I couldn't seem to help myself when I had a passing thought: *"God even has **cute** ones!"*

Before moving on with the completion of my story in this part one book, I must pause to mention the following: I was amazed again by how God does things to remind us that He is, in fact, **THE MAN**. The young, loving lady, Angelina, who blessed me with her spiritual warmness as I left the church that night, has a very similar name as the woman of God— Angela—whom God put in my life to complete this book. Even more astonishing is that her husband's first and last name is nearly identical to my first and middle name: James Edward. They are, of course, Mr. and Mrs. James and Angela Edwards.

While that Wednesday evening at the church was an amazing yet necessary experience at that very critical time in my life, I knew I couldn't trust my sons to remain in my home while not wanting to lose out on being healed from 22 years of drug use. I was stuck in the middle, all while wanting to aid them in their ongoing street recklessness and getting into constant trouble out there. God stepped in and brought me through it all — despite my still being unsure how to go about fixing the situation with my sons and making sure I kept my appointment for the hospital that coming Friday...a mere two days away. Later that night, right after that great 116th Street spiritual experience, I stopped at the liquor store to buy a bottle of wine. I was still disturbed. Then, I drove to my A.R.T.C. program, parked my taxi, and drank the entire bottle of Thunderbird. After throwing the Bible in the back seat that was given to me by the church's organ player, I then went to sleep.

The following morning, I went inside the building and talked to my counselor, sharing all the turmoil I was enduring and the amazing church experience. Being a former addict himself and a church-goer, he empathized with me and stated, *"You are done here and have been shifted to Morris Bernstein Hospital to finish your care, so let nothing stop you — including your two sons. God is in charge, not you."* Before letting me go, he quoted the following words of Jesus:

"The thief comes only to steal and kill and destroy. I have come that they may have life and have it to the full" (John 10:10, NIV).

From there, I went straight home and asked my sons to leave, which they did.

On October 22, 1980, after successfully completing my detox, I was officially drug-free and have never looked back.

CHAPTER 11: THE LEGENDARY TEENAGERS

At the time of this writing, there are two living legends of Frankie Lymon and The Teenagers: Herman Santiago and me, Jimmy Merchant. In 1981, we were back together on the stage as "The Legendary Teenagers." Instantly, we received worldwide attention—but before that, Herman and I had a very serious conversation centered around never giving up as a team, due to our group's name brand and our powerful, exceptional hit song, *Why Do Fools Fall in Love*.

Knowing something about his personality and how he viewed things differently that the other two Teenagers—Sherman and especially Joe saw—I didn't want things between us to fall apart. After all, we were back in touch with one another, basically "from the dead" (musically speaking), and were in contact with people in the music industry. After seriously considering a re-forming of The Teenagers, Herman said, *"Let's do it"*—and we did.

One of the first people I spoke to about the idea was our singing Italian friend, Eddy Rezzonico. He told me about a very popular deejay, Ronnie I, who was a very busy Doo-Wop New Jersey gentleman.

Herman and I began attending his dancehall events and socializing with singers there, even taking my son Solideen with me on the weekends. One of the top-flight lead singers I spoke to and set up an audition with at Herman's apartment was Ronnie Stewart (I'm still in touch with him today and often laugh about how things went). Another was Ray Wilson, whom I'm also still in touch with and always talk with about God. He, in fact, was in the group I began forming at A.R.T.C. and did the Don K. Reed Radio Show interview at that time.

In the end, Herman and I chose the dynamite female lead singer we had used in 1973: Ms. Pearl McKinnon. Out of the clear blue, the knowledgeable musical and Doo-Wop business gentleman, Joel Warshaw, aided Herman and me with getting the ball rolling with Pearl as well as our show on February 21, 1981. A note of importance is that Joel and Ronnie I worked to raise money for Frankie Lymon's never-gotten tombstone when he passed away. In 2020, Joel also aided Pam Nardella, who held onto the tombstone in her yard after Ronnie I passed, in getting it turned over to Mr. Gary "Dr. J" Johnson as the centerpiece for his new museum's Michigan Rock and Roll Legends Hall of Fame exhibit.

In closing, the point here is this: Regardless of where we are in life, we must know that God has a plan for each of us. He is constantly working on us by way of His love being transferred to our hearts to be utilized toward others, even moreso in these difficult days. I stop to reflect on the woman who questioned in her love note, *"Why do fools fall in love?"* The answer to that question is plain and clear where God is concerned. Like that woman, God loves us all, regardless of the foolishness in life that we go through. I also pause to think about all those times my life was spared before first accepting Jesus in 1980, and mainly in 1985.

If we have faith that can move mountains but have no love, we are nothing. Love is not what we say, love is what we do. The scriptures tell us:

"Love is patient, love is kind. It does not envy, it does not boast, it is not proud. It does not dishonor others, it is not self-seeking, it is not easily angered, it keeps no record of wrongs. Love does not delight in evil but rejoices with the truth. It always protects, always trusts, always hopes, always perseveres. Love never fails" (1 Corinthians 13:4-8a).

And so, as I end my thoughts in this first book of two of my life story, I still humbly cannot get over being gifted with superior fame beginning in 1956. It all began with "A Teenager's Dream." My dream is about God's purpose, calling, and destiny. I am one of five teenage boys who left a deep musical imprint on the world for 18 months with seven two-sided top-flight Rock 'n Roll / Pop hit songs that started with *Why Do Fools Fall in Love* — and, of course, God's Love.

Amen.

I am

Mr. James "Jimmy" Merchant
of the
Legendary "The Teenagers"

DISCOGRAPHY

Frankie Lymon and The Teenagers | *Gee Records*

- ❖ December 1955: *Why Do Fools Fall in Love* and *Please Be Mine*
- ❖ February 1956: *Love is a Clown, Am I Fooling Myself Again, I Want You to Be My Girl,* and *I'm Not a Know-It-All*
- ❖ May 1956: *Who Can Explain* and *I Promise to Remember*
- ❖ August 1956: *The ABCs of Love, Share, I'm Not a Juvenile Delinquent,* and *Baby Baby.*
  - o Interestingly, Juvenile Delinquent (the group's 5th release) was completed on August 4th with just The Teenagers. Frankie was later brought in to overdub the song in October.
- ❖ October 1956: *Paper Castles* and *Teenager Love*
- ❖ February 1957: *Out in the Cold Again* (The Teenagers only), *Miracle in the Rain, Little White Lies, Together, You, It Would Be So Nice, I Was Alone, Fortunate Fellow,* and *Love Put Me Out of My Head.*
  - o Miracle in the Rain was the flipside of Out in the Cold Again, with just Frankie singing.

- **May 1957:** *Begin the Beguine, You Can't Be True, Goodie Goodie,* and *Creation of Love.*
  - Frankie Lymon and The Teenagers recorded the last two songs, but Creation of Love was done over by Frankie alone. When the song was released, it lacked the version with The Teenagers' backup. That ushered in the end of the group and the beginning of Frankie's solo career.
- **August 1957:** *Lost Without Your Love* and *I'll Walk Alone.*
  - The Teenagers still had performances on the calendar but no lead singer. Billy Lubrano joined the group. He was half-Lain and in the same age range as the rest of The Teenagers.
- **November 1957:** *Flip-Flop* and *Everything to Me*
- **March 1958:** *Good Love, Mom I Wanna Rock,* and *My Brave Heart.*
- **March 1960:** *Crying* and *Tonight's the Night* (on End Records without Billy Lubrano).
  - Joe Negroni sang the lead; Kenny Bobo was added to the group.
- **June 1960:** *Can You Tell Me* and *A Little Wiser Now.*
  - Johnny Houston sang the lead.
- **March 1961:** *What's on Your Mind, Love Me Long,* and *He's No Lover.*

- o Joe Negroni sang the lead for What's on Your Mind.
- ❖ May 1961: *The Draw, I Heard the Angels Cry, The Wild Female,* and *Jean of the Ville.*
  - o Sherman Garnes sang the lead for The Draw (the group dressed as cowboys to sell the song).

Notably, The Teenagers recorded many other songs without Frankie Lymon but with other lead singers — male and female — throughout the years.

ABOUT THE AUTHOR

Born and raised in the Bronx, New York, **Jimmy Merchant** is best known for his contributions to music as an original founding member of the Doo-Wop vocal group Frankie Lymon and The Teenagers, and the co-writer of their greatest hit song, *Why Do Fools Fall in Love.*

In January 1956, Frankie Lymon and The Teenagers exploded onto the music scene with their first million-selling song that Jimmy inspired from a love letter titled "Why Do Birds Sing So Gay." Formed in a New York City junior high school, the street-corner serenading youths became superstars overnight. Their unique style and sound ushered in the "Kiddie Vocal Group Craze" and youth movement in music that resonates with music artists of today. New York Daily News' music historian, David Hinckley, wrote, "Before *Why Do Fools Fall in Love*, music was aimed at adults by adults. Suddenly, kids started making music for kids."

Jimmy has performed globally and in PBS music specials, television commercials, and on-screen movies. He also starred as himself in an off-Broadway musical that he co-wrote about his group. He was also honored as a Music Consultant by the Newark Black Film Festival in Newark, New Jersey, for a 1985 TV documentary about his group, which received the Paul Robeson Award for Excellence in Independent Filmmaking. The documentary was named after one of his group's hits: "Promise to Remember."

Jimmy is a member of the Vocal Group Hall of Fame, the Doo-Wop Hall of Fame of America, and others. In 1993, he and his group were inducted into the Rock and Roll Hall of Fame. The all-male R&B group, Boyz II Men, did the honors after singing *Why Do Fools Fall in Love* acapella.

Why Do Fools Fall in Love has been recorded by many others, including The Beach Boys and Diana

Ross, since its chart-breaking debut in 1956. The incomparable Diana Ross kept the song's pump primed in 1981, which became the subject matter and title for a 1998 movie about Frankie Lymon, starring Larenz Tate and Academy Award Winner Halle Berry. In 2001, The Recording Industry of America & The National Endowment for the Arts announced *Why Do Fools Fall in Love* as one of the "365 Songs of the Century."

Born with musical gifts to sing, hear, and arrange harmony, Jimmy Merchant's "DREAM" to perform has been accomplished beyond measure. Today, he is a vocal group master, a '50s Icon, and a Living Legend. Backed by other well-known group singers, he sang his dramatic, jaw-dropping original slow version of *Why Do Fools Fall in Love* — an addition to his self-produced 20-track Doo-Wop classic CD for collectors. In 2015, he re-recorded the up-tempo version of the song with Boyz II Men. The group Take Six assisted as Jimmy sang the bass line.

Additionally, one of the many talents Jimmy possesses is his ability to draw. Constant observation, practice, and studying the masters — which, he says, the "essentials" are based — enables him to work in all mediums, including collages. His portraits elicit various emotions, including his pencil portrait of Bill "Bojangles" Robinson, which was sold from a newspaper ad for a former show at the Art Institute & Gallery in Salisbury, Maryland, where he was also an instructor.

This Rock 'n Roll Hall of Famer still performs and has broadened his reach to win souls for Christ through his teaching and preaching as a minister of the Gospel and born-again Christian. His awe-inspiring testimony is consistent: He is blessed with a musical ability that enables him to touch the hearts and lives of humankind through his work that began as a dream from God. Jimmy has remained active in the music industry throughout his life, performing with other doo-wop groups and collaborating with other artists.

Jimmy and his beautiful wife, Mary, reside in the Bronx, New York. He is a proud father of six, devoted grandfather of 17, doting great-grandfather of 17, loving uncle, friend to many, and trusted confidant. Despite the ups and downs of his life and career, Jimmy's contributions to the golden age of Doo-Wop music and beyond will always be remembered.

To contact Jimmy Merchant for interviews, speaking engagements, and live performances, he can be reached at JimmyMerchant5@outlook.com.

Jimmy Merchant

WHY DO FOOLS FALL IN LOVE – SHEET MUSIC

WHY DO FOOLS FALL IN LOVE

Words and Music by MORRIS LEVY
and FRANKIE LYMON

A Teenager's Dream

Jimmy Merchant

Words and Music by MERRILL E. LAY and FRANKIE LYMON - WHY DO FOOLS FALL IN LOVE

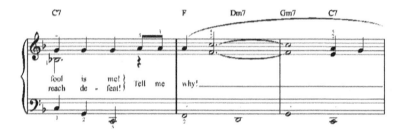

A Teenager's Dream

Stay tuned for the exciting continuation of Jimmy Merchant's historical account of his life-changing testimony:

A Teenager's Dream:
Being Prepared
(by and)
For God

A Teenager's Dream

Made in the USA
Las Vegas, NV
10 October 2024